DRAGONFLY

choosing to be nomads in retirement

MARGARET HERLE

One Printers Way
Altona, MB R0G 0B0
Canada

www.friesenpress.com

Copyright © 2024 by Margaret Herle
First Edition — 2024

This is my impression of what I saw, what I learned, what I thought.

You can contact the author at
mherlegilbert@gmail.com

ISBN
978-1-03-919258-4 (Hardcover)
978-1-03-919257-7 (Paperback)
978-1-03-919259-1 (eBook)

1. BIOGRAPHY & AUTOBIOGRAPHY, PERSONAL MEMOIRS

Distributed to the trade by The Ingram Book Company

To my late husband John

Many thanks to everyone who was part of these years,
and to those who are in my life now

Table of Contents

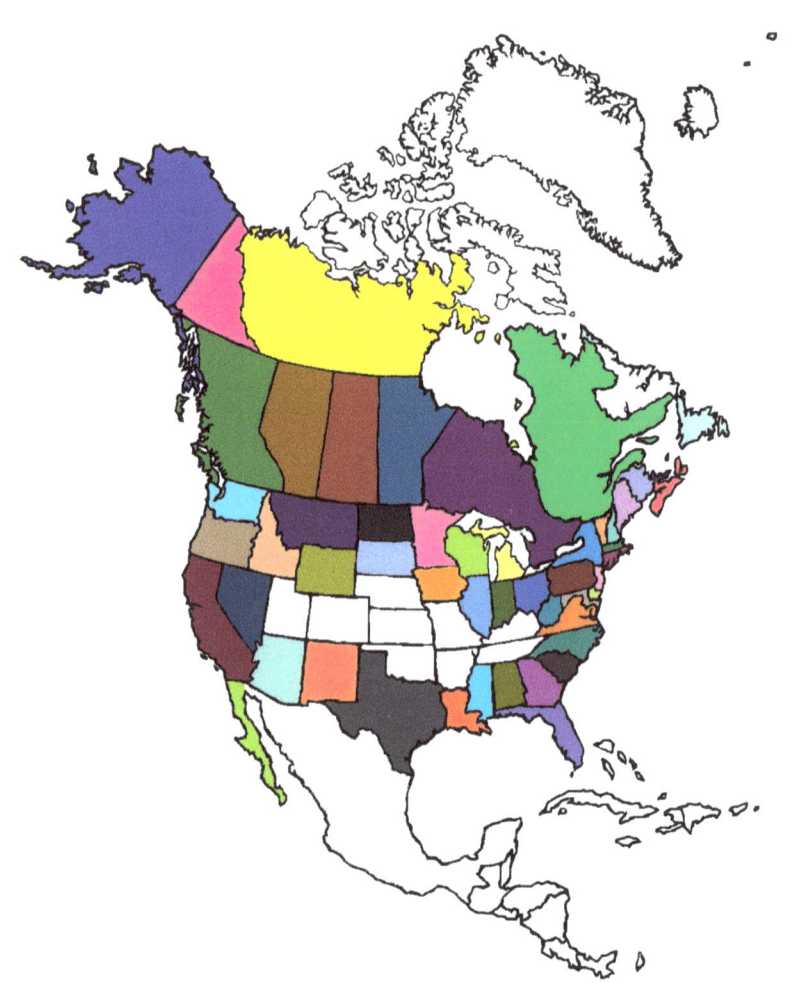

Preface

Now, as I complete this as a book, the world has changed so much, so fast, in the thirty-plus years since John and I began our life on wheels, and I'm realizing the similarities with the current trends of living in a van or in a tiny home, working remotely. I guess I could say we have done that, in the only way we knew then.

I wrote newsletters after each milestone trip and sent them out by mail to our families, friends, and neighbours, so that we kept in touch while John and I lived the dream of being able to travel in a way we could afford.

After I assembled these writings, I also realized that my book is a tribute to the strengths of John. There is no way I could have lived these adventures without him. I would never have bought a bus, built a motorhome within it, driven the bus, maintained the vehicle, or many of the jobs I saw him do.

I was the willing, happy partner, good navigator, great cook, housewife—to the best of my abilities, just as he did his best. Together we learned about places, people, geography, and made so many memories to share.

We were far from perfect, but decided on this meandering lifestyle, stuck to it, and had a great life together.

Now, the purpose of making this book available to anyone wanting to read it, is to invite you along for the ride as we experienced our retirement years on the road, connecting with people, places, and events far better than we could have imagined.

This is not intended as a guide for anyone choosing this lifestyle, but to show you, the reader, the endless possibilities and joys—and frustrations too—you might experience if you just dare to make your dreams happen. You have to do your research and look into what's possible today compared with what we managed to accomplish in our pioneering efforts. Still, I hope you take this book as inspiration and encouragement.

Some of the stories come from my original newsletter and thus appear as written, left in the present and/or various tenses as written and unchanged. Keep in mind also there was no email, no computers, or cell phones yet. We depended on pay phones, prepaid phone cards, and the postal service.

Some of this shared story is quite personal. Being part of a large wonderful family surely contributes to our way of life. So, after you meet and trust us, come on board and experience those wonderful years as I lived them. Hopefully, you might get some ideas and add some places to go on your own—whether or not you are in an RV.

#

The full value of the decision my husband and I made to live in a motorhome for retirement has become more obvious as time goes on. It was an honour and a privilege to be a tourist for so many years with the freedoms we had. To travel is such an incomparable education and I hope that those who want to travel, do it. Don't put it off too long. If ordinary people like John and I can find a way to do what we did, you too can make your dreams come alive—if you dare—as we did. Of course, John was not an ordinary guy, as you will see. He was skilled in so many ways that enabled his retirement dreams to come true.

I was a brand new graduate nurse on my first job in my home town of Camrose, Alberta. I was 21 years old, working shifts at the local hospital. My co-worker, Tina, wanted to introduce me to a fellow who worked with her husband in construction, saying that she had known this nice young man for years. She said, "I've already introduced him to other girls here. He hasn't been impressed by any of them, but I really think you two would like each other."

She continued to say so many nice things about him that in spite of the ten-year age difference, John sounded like a man I'd like to meet. She set us up on a blind date in December 1961.

Ooh, what a nice first impression when we met! Standing at my door was this tall, slim, neatly dressed man in a winter overcoat, with dark wavy hair, dark eyes, and such a pleasant shy smile. We spent the whole evening just sitting, chatting, getting to know each other. He happened to be off work for a few days, so we made a date to see each other again the next night, and the next and the next.

Tina was right! He was such a nice person, our evenings flew by, just chatting so easily. In only about three weeks, I think we both knew we cared a whole lot about each other. We shared so many values that we already felt that we should be married one day. We were so confident the essentials to a happy life were there.

In the next few months, we saw each other as often as we could, mainly only on weekends. He was a backhoe operator for a construction company that took him to different towns to dig service lines. Usually they were too far away for the crew to come home every day, so they would find room and board in each town where the job was.

We learned that we both grew up on farms and came from big families. He definitely had a tougher upbringing than me. His young years were in Saskatchewan during the Depression that started in 1930, the year he was born. He had no memory of ever having toys; he would just kick a can, play with a stick, sift sand or dirt through his fingers. But mostly there was work to do and no time to play anyway.

For him, summers always passed too quickly, and he hated the winters. He said he was SO COLD all winter. His shoulders would be scrunched up for hours making his muscles ache from being so tense until he could eventually relax them by a warm stove or in a warm room. Later, when we were married, I recall feeling sorry for him as he would lay on the floor by a warm heat register when he came in from the cold.

His class attendance during his school years was governed by whether or not he was needed at home or in the fields, so he quit school at age 14 and had worked ever since. His family did not include the love it should have, like mine certainly did. His father died when John was 21, leaving several young ones at home with their mother on the farm. John had just three days off work for bereavement to attend his dad's funeral. At that time, he was working in the Athabasca region of northern Alberta, cutting through bush on a caterpillar on tracks, making roads for the working crews that would follow.

We both grew up in large Catholic families, and we both wanted a family life filled with love and children. Earlier, I had wanted to be a nun in an orphanage so I could have lots of children to care for. When I said I wanted fourteen kids, John wasn't scared. He was the second of eleven, I was the eldest of nine, so lots of kids sounded just fine. Together, we had EIGHTEEN brothers and sisters! We had so many easy conversations about our pasts, and what we would like for the future.

A girlfriend and I shared a basement suite close to the hospital, and one memorable night John was our literal Batman who rescued us when we called him in a panic to come over and get rid of the bat in our place. Sally had wrapped a pair of her pants around her head so the bat couldn't get tangled in her hair like in the stories she'd heard. John was definitely our hero when he ushered the bat out the door with a broom!

Sandy, boyfriend of my roommate, my roommate Sally, myself and John. Note the rotary phone on the wall.

Despite his difficult childhood, John continually surprised me with his sense of humour—dry, wry, witty. He also had an amazingly keen sense of finances and numbers. He said he had always loved to read, teaching himself so much through books. He wanted so badly to learn to fly a plane, but the resources were never there.

My sister Rose and her fiancé, Tony, were already engaged at this time, and John thought it wouldn't be right to interfere with their plans, so we waited to be engaged. However, just two weeks after their wedding in July, John gave me a diamond ring and my poor parents had to make another wedding that summer. In those days, if you wanted to get married, you did just that. There was no waiting a year or so to make those plans. It was a community event, enjoyed by all. And in my small town of Round Hill, everyone gets involved and invited; there were no small weddings. Ours was September 29, 1962, during harvest season!

Our honeymoon was a road trip from Camrose to the World's Fair in Seattle. The travel curiosity was already there, and I got to learn and hone my good navigational skills.

John already owned a lovely old house for us to live in, one of those with hardwood floors and a lovely veranda across the entire front of it. He still often had to work out of town during the week, so we were together mostly on weekends. Not the nicest arrangement, but that's how it had to be.

Our first home

Soon, our first baby was expected, and life was so good. I worked full time, sometimes during some precious hours that John would be home on a weekend.

John's sister Hilda was getting married in July the next year. Their wedding date was on the due date for our first baby. As the older brother, John was giving the bride away. During Hilda's wedding, I started having discomfort strong enough that I went to the hospital before the reception. I needed something to ease the pain and, being a nurse, I figured the first baby would arrive past the due date and I wanted to enjoy the reception. Well, upon examination, it was determined that I was already in labour, so I told John, "You go to the reception, because it will probably be a few hours for a first baby."

About an hour later, I was wheeled into a room with a phone so I could call John at the reception and tell him we had a baby girl! He said when the staff called him to the kitchen to take a phone call, you could have heard a pin drop, then he came out beaming, "It's a girl!" So fast! He said he was so proud to tell the wedding party that he had given away a Miss Herle in the morning and now he had another Miss Herle!

We were bursting with pride at our accomplishment when he came back to the hospital to see his little family. The grandparents came too, and it was such a happy wedding dance they returned to. So much to celebrate!

Since I worked at the hospital, I knew most of the people in the area. Still, I was surprised and had to laugh when, a few days later, one of the other new moms came in to my room to say that some of them saw us when we came into the hospital. John had been wearing a boutonnière and I was dressed up as if for a wedding, so they all wanted to know "Were we were just married on that day?"

Four months later, we learned we were having a second baby. Fantastic!

That January was particularly cold in the small town in southern Alberta where John was working with his crew, digging lines for water and sewer installations. It was so cold that straw and coal fires had to be kept burning all night along the frozen ground so digging would be easier in the morning. John was foreman for that job and, of course, let the crew warm up for a few minutes as a break, but when the boss drove into town one day and saw that, he said, "Johnny, I saw those guys just standing there, warming their hands. You can't let them do that." That was the last straw for John. He quit. He could not be cruel to his crew. The working conditions were not good. He had tried to quit before, but had been talked into doing this one last job.

He was REALLY, REALLY wanting to get out of this job and the COLD, COLD winters sitting on a COLD, COLD machine. We packed up our belongings, bought a new pickup truck, found renters for the house, stored half our belongings at his sister Irene's house in Calgary, loaded up the rest, and headed for Vancouver. Hilda and Denis, the newlyweds, were already there. We had visited with them on our honeymoon and talked about relocating even then.

My parents cried as we drove away with their first granddaughter, because "over the mountains" was such a long ways away. That's how we came to live in British Columbia in February of 1964.

When it was time for our second baby to be born, my sister Lucy came from Edmonton to stay for the event. She had to extend her holidays because that little one wasn't ready yet! On June 20, we had Allan—a brother for Karen before her first birthday. How beautiful!

Most jobs in John's line of work were unionized, so it was very tough on us. The union wouldn't accept John's membership because he didn't have a regular job, and he couldn't get a construction job because he didn't have a union card! There was much frustration for many weeks. John's brother George came to BC too and stayed with us. We learned to value every penny we had among us.

One of John's early jobs was erecting steel fencing around the docks at Prince Rupert, 900 miles north of Vancouver. He was gone a couple weeks. On the way home the company truck went off the slippery road in the Fraser Canyon and rolled down an embankment. I got a call from him from the hospital in Hope, a couple of hours away, to say he was okay. He had a badly twisted and sprained ankle and lots of bruises, but the accident had made the news on the radio and he didn't want me to hear about it that way first. Apparently, as the truck flipped end over end a couple times, John was thrown under the dash, all curled up with ground glass in his hair, skin, clothes. His boss didn't fare as well, and was crushed in the chest by the steering wheel. They were both lucky to be alive. When John and his brother George went to see the location later, they found John's shoe that had been knocked off in the accident.

The damaged truck

Hilda and Denis were the only other relatives we knew in the Vancouver area, so we alternated dinners on Sundays and kept in close touch. We also met and enjoyed our neighbours, John and Carol Sinkie, who became lifelong friends and accepted our "Kool-Aid" and popcorn during visits because we couldn't afford beer. Our two little families sure did have a lot of fun together.

When Allan was four months old, we were pregnant with our third baby, and life was full and happy. At the end of July, Keith was born. He had dark hair, different from Karen and Allan, who had such lightly coloured tops. We just kept on being so busy, so satisfied with our family! Karen was just past her second birthday when she had these two younger brothers. I said it was my summer vacation, being in hospital for a week each of the three summers! It was wonderful because we all grew up together, even if there were about five years of blur for John and me.

Our little family

Allan, Keith, Karen

Through friends, we found an acreage in Richmond to rent. It had a big fenced yard for our little ones to play in and a bountiful garden already growing beside the house. There was a good barn on the property, so John was able to use his farming skills. He would buy very young calves at auctions to feed and care for so he could sell them at a profit later. At this time, he was working an afternoon shift at a plywood plant. At times, it was a struggle to feed all of us—as well as buy feed for our calves—but in spite of that we knew we had made the right move for us.

The winters were SO much better for John than in Alberta and Saskatchewan. As John said, he eventually bought himself a job. After working for others as much as he could, he bought an old backhoe and looked for more hourly work, advertising in the Yellow Pages—the business section—of the phone book, which was the typical thing to do then when you had a company.

Our first rental house in Richmond

Work was spotty but John worked hard to find jobs, and even got contracts for snow removal from parking lots for a few businesses. We never thought we'd pray for snow, since he HATED SNOW AND COLD, but we needed the work, and he spent many tired, cold, and slippery hours doing snow removal during those winters.

We had a great garden both at that acreage and the next rental, also in Richmond. But before the kids started school, we found a house we could buy in Burnaby. This was so exciting for me! I wanted to kiss the floors and the glass in the windows that now belonged to us!

That first rental house in Richmond was built on cement blocks and had so many huge spiders that I called them Elephant Pete! I swear I could hear them walking. When the babes were all in bed, I sometimes sat in an armchair waiting for John to come home from his afternoon shift at the plywood plant, with a can of Raid in one hand and a can of hairspray in the other. The hairspray would slow them down, the Raid made sure they never came back!

11

The second rental had a basement but NO CLOSETS! Finally, our third home in BC—and this first home we ever bought in BC—had closets and a full basement! We were rich now!

We were in a delightful neighbourhood in Burnaby with lots of kids, just before our own were old enough to go to school. Everybody knew everybody and had lots of fun. I remember a picture taken of various moms and kids out for bike rides together. Halloween was so much fun, the costumes all homemade, and loads of candies brought home!

The school years flew by. It was too far to send Karen alone to the Catholic school and she would have had to cross the busy street Kingsway, so we put her into the little public school and were glad we did. Being in the neighbourhood there was great.

A novel First Communion photo op

When an acre of raw forested land in the neighbourhood became available to us, we managed to buy and build our family home on it! Because John dug dirt so well, he shaped the steeply sloped lot and we worked hard to build ourselves a brand-new house! We had a twenty-year mortgage paid off in eight years by saving pennies again and not wanting to pay interest any more than was absolutely necessary. I think that was John's secret to success. Own what you have; don't let anyone else live off of you by paying interest to them. We saved THOUSANDS of dollars over the years this way. This included the early '80s, when interest rates were up to 19 percent. It had been second nature to us to be aware of every penny we spent. We never had a regular payday. We

13

always had to wait for a cheque in the mail and sometimes they took a long time to arrive.

We moved into our newest home well before the occupancy permit allowed, with bare plywood floors, without kitchen appliances—we used an electric frying pan because there was no kitchen stove yet—and no interior doors. But all was done in good time. We were so delighted with owning our own home, and worked very hard to get it built.

Sure, there were rough patches in our lives but, between John and I, the goal was to stick together forever. We knew that we trusted each other implicitly even as we argued or watched friends separate.

John didn't get an opportunity to go far in school. He was self-taught and learned life lessons the hard way, so it was most important to him to give our kids the very best education we could. We planned to support them as long as they were students, but had to change our minds and quit the financial support of tuition after they reached their Bachelor's Degrees. We had no savings account at all in those days. Life used all of it! With all three kids in university, they were forming their own lives. We had an accountant, an engineer, and a hopeful medical student with great educations that their father could never dream of. That was his legacy to his children!

So many family events happened along the years. Our twenty-fifth anniversary was well celebrated with almost complete attendance of our family, along with many friends. That was a beautiful occasion and a happy milestone.

A year later, Karen and her beau, Serge, called from Montréal to announce their engagement! Their wedding was planned to take place in Burnaby, and they came from Montréal for that special day in May 1990.

Proud father of the bride in 1990.

15

Our grownup children: Keith, Karen, Allan.

I loved that Marine Drive home in Burnaby so much that I wanted to live there forever and have our kids and their families live with us, but I had learned another two important things from John by that time:

1. Be grateful that our kids could make it on their own.

2. We couldn't afford to live there when John retired. He would have had to keep on working, and felt that he just couldn't do it much longer. He said that construction was a younger man's game, not for someone his age any more. He had already lost friends in their early 60s. He felt that he would never make it if he had to work until 65.

His goal had been "freedom 55," when he wanted to drive over his lunch bucket with his backhoe and never have to eat another sandwich, but a downturn in the economy kept him working an extra four years for less wages.

John's retirement goal was always to spend winters in the warm south. After living in our house for seventeen years, it was time to make a move to something smaller that we could afford in retirement.

For us, vacations always had to be inexpensive. Mostly we drove to Alberta for visits with family and the friends we'd left behind. During our working years, we managed some short January trips to Mexico to enjoy some of that warmer winter weather, and some brief trips to California and Arizona with a motorhome, which had replaced the small trailer that had replaced the tent that introduced us to camping when our kids were very young.

During our first winter trip to Mexico in the mid-1970s, John had really wanted to experience the country and its people by bus. Through a travel agent, we booked a flight south to the sunshine in San Francisco where we would then continue by bus to Mexico City. In San Francisco, we visited my cousin Amelia and her husband Leon. I had a special closeness to her because, as a teen, I had been the recipient of some of her lovely clothes—much nicer than what I had. From there, we went by bus to Las Vegas (visited family friends there), Los Angeles and San Diego (taking Gray Line bus tours in both cities), Tijuana, and continued for twenty-seven hours on the bus to Mazatlan, Guadalajara, and Mexico City for a few days each before we flew home. We were quite the greenhorns, but loved the travels! Even though we'd been warned to take toilet paper with us for use at the bus stops—which we did—unfortunately it was in a suitcase under the bus for the twenty-seven-hour ride to Mazatlan, so we still had to pay the pesos for the coarse or sometimes "half-ply" that was given to us. For the second trip, we studied more Spanish so we could do better than hold out our palms with some pesos in them to let the merchants take what was owed when we bought items along the way. Never did anyone ridicule us, or make us feel uncomfortable. This time we were climbing pyramids, sightseeing, going to new places, and having exciting experiences while enjoying winter warmth and sunshine.

We had always wanted to travel much more, to see this great continent of ours, to spend more time in winter warmth and sunshine, but we would not be able to afford a home and still travel as planned in retirement, so we thought maybe we should just sell our big house and travel a bit BEFORE we bought the smaller home. Spending warm winters was always a part of the plan.

At that time, around 1987, John's brother George happened to be driving a highway bus, and he knew someone who was doing a bus conversion, transforming it into a beautiful motorhome. We talked about possibly doing that ourselves, and then we could live in it while we travelled! We had our ideal solution. John knew if it was built in a quality way, we could be very happy in it and it would have value as a down payment for our next home. We could travel maybe one to ten years, or until one of us wasn't having fun any more.

Some friends thought this was a crazy idea, but it was what we decided to do. An RV would depreciate over the years, but the bus conversion could keep a lot of value!

This was not the typical thing for Canadians to do at that time, but we weren't the typical Canadian couple—nor were we the first ones with this idea.

John was very capable of creating and doing many things, including building, diesel mechanics, and welding. To learn more, we subscribed to a trailer magazine and joined the Family Motor Coach Association. We learned about brands, floor plans, new inventions, people's comments, and so much more. We studied floor plans: I loved the aesthetics and comments,

John was all in for the engines, power, mileages, and all the mechanical issues. We attended RV shows, started seriously considering buying a bus, and ended up with a 1973 forty-foot Vancouver-based tour bus.

Once that final decision was made, there was no going back for us. We had it parked in our backyard with the intention of completing it in one year, even though more experienced people told us it would take longer. We said, "No, we are the Herles and we plan to do it in a year!"

When we told the kids we were going to live in a bus, they said, "Yes! Can we paint it like the Partridge Family bus?" We said, "Thanks, but no thanks, this is our Herle family bus!" We would decide on a design together a little later.

The original bus colour.

Herle Excavating Ltd.

Stripped bare inside bus

Eventually, John sold his backhoe business and worked full time on this project so he could spend winters away from the cold … as soon as possible! He had begun by removing all the seats, the washroom, and stripping the entire interior to the bare frame. We used masking tape on the floor to mark the rooms, the counters, the nook—all the divisions needed—to help us visualize our space.

There were special features, such as the toe space in front of the cabinets and hot-water heating instead of forced air. I could never accept nor understand why, in those very pricey factory-built motorhomes, the forced air vents were right in the middle of the floor.

John kept working as hard as he could, determining all the electrical, plumbing, and heating lines needed. Holes were cut in the roof for vents that would later become places for the air conditioners, and we hired a plumber, an electrician, and a guy who did the spray foam insulation. We were now building, not taking apart, and it was becoming more real!

We hired a boat builder to build the solid-oak cabinets. Not only were the sides of the bus curved but the roof-line was as well, so each piece had to be scribed and cut individually. It was taking shape! For the winter, John assembled a tarp to cover the entire length of the bus and workspace and, with a little heater inside, work continued every day.

Then, one night I was suddenly jarred awake by John having a grand mal seizure during his sleep. I called 911 and suddenly six strangers were in our bedroom, carrying him out. After a short stay in hospital, followed by a very severe reaction to a medication that made him tired and sore, gave him blotchy skin, and had him limping for a few weeks, he was unable to help the carpenter much during that time. No definite cause for the seizure was found, but I believed it was his undiagnosed sleep apnea.

We learned that plans can be derailed at any time. But we always had a Plan B and, if needed, Plan C, even if sometimes we were on Plan J! Together we were determined to work through or around to a solution!

My cousin Don Keller and his wife Diane joined in to help with so much. Diane became my decorator/helper/buddy. After the bathtub, counter-tops, and fixture colours were chosen, we'd go shopping for upholstery fabrics, carpeting, and planning the decor. Our colours were dusty pink for counter-tops, burgundy for furniture, grey for bathroom fixtures, a tweedy combination of burgundy and grey for carpet, and a lovely patterned white linoleum in the kitchen and bathroom. It was gorgeous. As the cabinets were taking shape, our boat-builder/cabinet builder taught us about using three different dilutions of marine varnish in between gentle sanding of each piece. There were twenty-seven doors and drawers that got individual attention, all spread out on the ping-pong table in the basement rec room of our home.

Since John had ten brothers and sisters and I had eight, we wanted to have space for family visits too, so we needed good and comfortable accommodations that would last. And because we might sometimes argue or disagree (oh yes, we do), we had included separate spaces so we could manage that too. There was a TV at the front and another one in the comfy back bedroom. We learned along the way that the bedroom should be beautiful because if one of us wanted to be alone or had sick days, it wouldn't be in a dark or dingy room.

The exterior design was sleek and the painting was done the following summer in our backyard. When the masking paper came off to reveal the design, it was as if we'd unwrapped the biggest gift ever!

The bus being unwrapped.

John said he apologized to our bus as it stood outside in the snow for a second winter, with its fresh coat of paint. He said it was pawing at the dirt, ready for the warmer winters it had been promised instead of this snow and cold.

bus covered in snow

Almost two years after we bought the bus, the house was sold and the garage sales were over but the bus still wasn't quite finished. Fortunately, we were able to rent our own house for two more months after it was sold, as we emptied it and filled the bus. A new white Honda Civic car was added to the bus with a hitch and a tow bar. A rear camera was installed so we could easily check on the car still being with us. Finally, the guys took the bus on a little test run, checked the tires, filled the fuel and water tanks, and everything was ready to go. John said he hoped he wouldn't need a little trailer to haul all my Tupperware!

We were proud of the new home with a fold-out double sofa-bed, convertible nook that could be a single bed, a lovely queen island bed for us, a full-size bathtub with shower, and even a little glass-door cabinet with an etched pattern by my brother Ken. It was everything we could wish for, including a four-burner stove and micro/convection oven—all within our forty-foot coach!

Finished at last!

When it was time to leave the house, I felt pride and relief rather than any sadness. We knew we had sold a quality home that we had built seventeen years before, and we were now moving into our new quality-built home on wheels that we had JUST built!

So, the great change of lifestyle had begun. I was still only fifty years old, and we were like giddy little kids again, off on our big adventure.

Our children were in their twenties, carving their own individual lives, and we were off to see the world—or at least most of North America! John and I were beginning our personal adventure of travelling North America in our own tour bus, towing our new little car behind us.

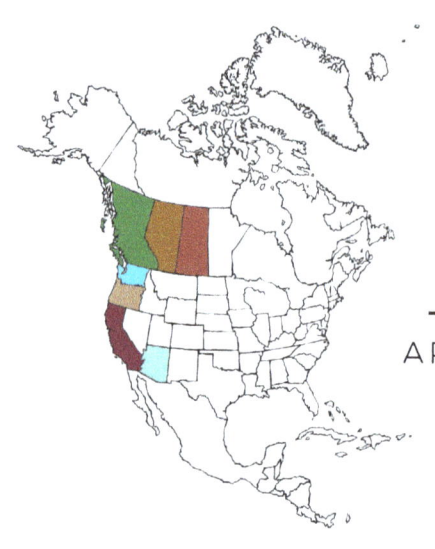

On the Road at Last: Rambling and Rallies

As we drove away from the house along the back lane, both of us were surprised when I told John that I suddenly realized I had never been a passenger in our new home until that moment! John had driven it home on the day of purchase while I followed in the car and, since then, it was only out of our backyard for servicing necessities. I hadn't driven in the bus during those preparatory rides; I was always plenty busy in the house.

On our way to the freeway, on narrow Front Street in New Westminster, he asked "What's wrong, why are you so nervous?" I said, "I'm not nervous, I trust your driving." I was totally unaware that I was pulling in my elbow every time we passed a telephone pole. Because I was sitting up so high and on the passenger side, I felt so close to the edge of the road, I guess I thought I'd have to

26

tuck in my elbow or it may be scraped! Already lesson number-one in relaxing!

Our first destination was Chilliwack for a couple of days at his brother Jerry's acreage to see if everything worked the way it should ... and it most certainly did!

The next stop was in Valemount, where we celebrated John's sixty-first birthday with a candle in a cupcake at a campground. It was May 1, 1991.

We were so excited to be on our way to my thirty-year nursing reunion near Edmonton, to be followed by a summer of introducing our new home-on-wheels to family and friends, including those who thought this was a crazy idea at first! We would show them the comfy new home where we would be living during our travels and warmer winters.

The nursing reunion was exciting—it's only every five years—but this time it wasn't too difficult to say goodbye to my friends so I could get back to John and the bus to continue our travels.

From then on we rambled all summer, visiting friends and family, through Alberta and then Saskatchewan. As soon as John felt the wind in Saskatchewan, he said, "Now I remember why I wanted to leave there so badly."

By fall we were in California, enjoying kiwis (twenty for a dollar!), pistachios, persimmons, olives, gorgeous new scenery, and a great life. My cousin Amelia and her husband Leon still lived in the San Francisco area and visited us at a nearby campsite, behind the levees of the Sacramento River. We thought that the American Thanksgiving weekend would be a good time of year to try be south by to avoid our Canadian winters.

So why is our bus called *Dragonfly*? On its maiden voyage to California, we were with our friends Irv and Nancy, also beginning full-timers from Surrey, leading in their Eagle bus. Both buses were labouring hard to conquer the Siskiyou Pass at Oregon's southern border, when we overheard one trucker ask another trucker on the CB , "Do you know what these old bus conversions following us are called?" "No," the second driver replied. The first trucker answered: "They are called dragonflies because they drag their asses up one side of the hill, then they fly down the other." That does describe us pretty well, and John and I liked the name. Nancy had something different in mind for their bus, so our *Dragonfly* was named.

Later, Jack Gleadle—another Surrey bus-conversion owner, friend, and accomplished artistic painter—wrote *Dragonfly* in beautiful letters on a piece of plexiglass that we attached to the front of the bus. His own bus was called *Flyin' High* because he was a bush pilot. I think his bus name might have been the reason for an intense customs check one time. He might have been erroneously suspected of "flyin' high" on something else but his years as a bush pilot had earned him that name.

Among our exciting new finds in California was cheaper meats. When we saw turkey for nine cents a pound, we couldn't believe it, so we bought a big one! Twenty-six pounds! We felt so stupid when we got back to *Dragonfly* and there was absolutely no way it would fit in the freezer! So, we put the bird in a cardboard box, stuffed newspapers around it, and put it in the trunk of the car. A couple days later, when we could pry off the drumsticks and wings, I cooked them and froze the meat in Ziploc baggies. We kept taking off parts of the turkey as we could, and had turkey soups and stews for most meals for a while, laughing at our necessary resourcefulness. We didn't waste anything, and spent very little on groceries for a while, so happy to be in the warmth of California and heading to Arizona!

We rambled in the Yuma area, spending time finding and connecting with those we knew were travelling through there at the same time, seeing date and citrus farms, and discovering how delicious a date shake is!

That first Christmas, we flew to Montréal to see Karen, Serge, and our first grandchild, Marc, who was such a beautiful cuddly baby. We so enjoyed playing with him! And in our luggage was a frozen turkey ... because, of course, they were so much cheaper in the US!

Our winters in Arizona were going to be so good. Our first month-long stay would be at the Sun Vista Resort in Yuma because John had a cousin, George Volk, there in a rental for the winter months, giving us lots of time to visit together. We quickly met and made many new friends with people enjoying their own warm winters. I wrote this letter home describing a surprisingly eventful life.

FEB 1992

Dear friends and family,

We are still debating whether or not we'll add another week to our month here at Sun Vista in Yuma, Arizona. The weather has been just great, and we're having such good times with the people around us. Except for the day before yesterday ...

There was to be a Family Motor Coach Association Rally in Casa Grande, about a three-and-a-half-hour drive east from here, and we wanted to go. We were looking forward to the seminars on maintenance, diesels, many topics pertaining to the RV life, and we were looking for a couple of accessories, and maybe even get an awning if prices were special.

Well, there's this fun couple, Paul Jones (PJ) and his wife BJ across from us here in this resort, and we would travel together. Another dear couple, Donna and Carlo, were on the working committee and left for Casa Grande three days earlier to help set up. About eight hundred RVs were expected. We had never ever experienced something like this!

So, the day before yesterday, we drove east, away from Yuma, in the sunshine, as happy as can be, chatting on the CB radio with PJ and BJ. Paul was telling us stories and history about the area, and BJ and I talked about the desert flowers beginning to bloom. She said the yellow blossoms sticking out of the bushy plants on the roadside here remind her of a birthday cake with candles lit.

John had done a good job of washing the engine a couple of days earlier and even put fresh paint on some engine parts because we hear that at these rallies you look at each others' engines and rigs a lot, too.

John still believes in Murphy's Law, yet he'd washed the motorhome in spite of saying it would rain when we travel—it usually does!

Well, we soon ran into rain. There had been some very recent major flooding in the Los Angeles area—it seems there was a series of storms like that going east. So far, all these storms have skipped right over Yuma. We've had some clouds and cooler days and a bit of rain a couple times. But, I'm straying a bit.

About three quarters of the way to our destination, it started to rain—just lightly at first. We drove to a factory outlet mall as a prearranged meeting place. We were an hour early, so we shopped a bit. Then, since there were no other motorhomes there yet, we inquired and learned we were at the wrong mall. We drove a little farther along Highway 10, to the correct mall, where we saw many motorhomes gathered. Via CB, we located two rigs belonging to the club that would take us under their wing because it was our first rally.

By now, rain was almost torrential at times and the skies were dark and low. Together, we four rigs drove the seven miles out toward the fairgrounds to the rally site, but drove right past the corner where we should have turned! So, all four motorhomes had to turn around at the next corner and go back the mile or so. It was really pouring buckets now!

We approached the site, and we could see that some parts of the fairgrounds were already under water. The parking directors were parking the rigs by backing them up against the fence, at right angles to the road. That meant the back end of most motorhomes would be a little lower than the front. We were directed to the next available spot and, with guidance, we backed in.

Already we were all wondering if we shouldn't leave and go home. Besides, it would be such a long walk into the fairgrounds through so much water and muddy sand. Well, we didn't have to wonder for long … There was a trench no one knew about until our back wheels rested in it. So there we were! We'd need a tow sooner or later, so it was quickly decided that we'd use our Good Sam Emergency Road Service now, just in case our situation got worse. PJ and John decided we'd go home as soon as we were pulled out and we'd forget about this rally.

I had cut up a garbage bag to make a temporary raincoat for BJ, then gave her my winter boots (she just had pretty pink runners with her) and loaned her an umbrella (I found three). Paul and John had huddled together under PJ's print umbrella and went to the buildings looking for a pay phone to call for the tow truck.

When they came back, John giggled and said he'd been worried what others may have thought of him huddled so close to another man under this pretty umbrella, but not worried enough to want to get wetter. He also said he'd kept PJ running back and forth getting the answers John needed for the tow service to get to us. It's a 1-800 phone number so he had no idea of where he was calling.

Of course, the exact address was needed, so it was obtained: Eleven Mile Corner, Pinal County Fairgrounds, Casa Grande,

Arizona. Then John was asked for the zip code. I'm not sure whether they eventually got that or not. Anyway, by the time the fellows got back, we knew we were leaving ASAP.

PJ is also a Good Sam Emergency Service member and he said he'd get towed out, too, if they were stuck. They weren't stuck, so they left and said they'd wait for us back at the mall where we'd come from. Then the tow truck came. More rigs were leaving all the time and the rain would deluge and stop. The road across from us was flooded, the fairgrounds were flooded, and the water in front of us was running faster and wider every time I looked.

When he arrived, the tow operator assessed the situation and decided to call the sheriff because the road would have to be blocked. Meanwhile, another rig in our group had reached PJ and BJ, and told them that our tow truck had arrived. We waited for the sheriff—the Jones's waited for us. Almost an hour later, the sheriff arrived, blocked the road with his car, lights flashing, and he went to the other side to just stand there to provide his official presence, as a rather large group of hooded, umbrella'd, wet, muddy individuals with smiles, looks of concern, cameras, video cameras, and bated breath had gathered to watch as we were soaked by deluges, then respites—brief ones!

The bus was winched out quite nicely—no problem. The tow truck and its operator were very capable. When we register with Good Sam, we register our vehicle type—so by our registration, Good Sam Service knew we were a bus conversion. [Good Sam Road Service is comparable to AAA or CAA, but for RVs, and has many member campgrounds as well.]

Dragonfly being towed out of the trench.

On our way back into town, we heard our friend Carlo call on the CB talking about the order of the afternoon for the rally. The reply sounded like the first seminar would be at four o'clock. It was called "Attitude Adjustment." Too bad we were on our way out. We sure could have used that seminar!!

As we drove away from the fairgrounds, we met PJ and BJ headed in the opposite direction!!! They said they'd waited so long after they were told the tow truck arrived, they were imagining all sorts of things had happened, so they were coming back to check on us. So, thanks to the CB again, we agreed to meet at a certain service station where Highway 10 and Highway 8 intersect, so we were told to go SOUTH on Highway 10. Right then, we'd reached the freeway exit, but there the signs said 10 EAST or WEST, not SOUTH. No time to think, so we took WEST—to get back to Yuma. We quickly realized we should have gone EAST! We turned around at the next interchange, but were out of CB range to Paul until we got near the intersection of Highways 10 and 8 again, and we were making our turn onto 8, toward home. We shouldn't have done that either. The meeting place was just a bit further on Highway 10. Via CB, we agreed to stay put and PJ would find us pronto. He did, and finally we were together—headed home!

Just as we got going again, two red warning lights started flashing and a warning buzzer sounded in our coach. HOT ENGINE and LOW OIL flashed. PJ didn't have his CB on, and we HAD to stop!!! About a half mile further, Paul noticed we'd stopped with our flashers on. I could hear them calling us on the CB, but there was so much static they couldn't hear me. There was no rain in this area, and hadn't been for just a few miles already. Slowly the Joneses backed up all the way to us.

By then, John had learned it wasn't an oil problem. A hose clamp had broken and we'd lost our antifreeze and water—maybe all thirty gallons—so he replaced the hose clamp and stood on a five-gallon bucket and reached way up to fill the radiator with a water hose hooked to our outside tap. Two positive things—installing the outside tap idea was invaluable, and John had filled our water tank before the trip. We felt better when the engine was started and everything was okay.

When John told Paul we'd just lost our rad water, Paul asked "What's a rad? Do I have one?" We sure laughed about the Canadian abbreviation for radiator. We were headed out to the Vija truck stop where we'd seen a good price on diesel fuel on our way through that morning. Oh, that seemed like so long ago!!

When we stopped there for lunch, it was almost 3:00 p.m. We'd been up since 5:30 a.m. and now that seemed like days ago. Both men looked really tired, and during lunch we realized we really didn't have to hurry any more. No one expected us back for two or three days and we were now back in sunshine. We'd left tornado warnings behind us, according to the radio, and we breathed a huge sigh of relief!

Funny what a difference a few miles and a few ridges of even these low mountain ranges can make in the weather. We drove maybe another thirty miles to a big McDonald's parking lot in Gila Bend, had a "Miller Time" break, held our own private "Attitude Adjustment" seminar and watched a beautiful sunset and let the darkness envelope us. Our buddies went to bed at 7:30 p.m., us at 8:30 p.m.

BJ, PJ, and John after a failed attempt to attend our first rally.

The next morning was Valentine's Day and we both felt like we'd been on the road for a week. Our boots had dried mud on them. Luckily, we had our leftover carpet scrap pieces to use for protecting our living room floor, and the umbrellas were propped near the driver's seat. About 6:30 a.m. we were having breakfast together at McDonald's and the rest of the way home was uneventful—especially after the previous day.

As we pulled up to our sites in Sun Vista, neighbours came over, concerned as to why we returned so soon.

I set the boots and carpet pieces outside to dry in the sun, and we just visited with our campground neighbours and enjoyed the sunshine while we explained our early return.

John says that was two rallies in one—his first and his last! But … we'll try to change his mind real quick. In fact, there's this group from here going to the Indio Date Festival in just three days, and the weather forecast in that westerly direction looks really good …

A FEW DAYS LATER

Well, we did go to that date festival, and had such a good time watching the ostrich races with the very hilarious commentating that kept us in stitches. John even got to ride a camel, which was funny on its own!

John on the camel.

One incident was very tense after the rally, when Carlo mistakenly filled his diesel tank with gasoline—a very dangerous thing to do. The fellows all helped to push his motorhome away from the gas pumps for safety, and we waited until some workers came along to drain the fuel tank so it could be refilled with clean diesel. We women realized the danger we were in by the frantic yelling and running and frustration we saw outside. Whew! Another lesson learned. Pay attention to what you are pumping!

Rushing to fill any containers they could find to empty the diesel/gasoline mixture from the tank of the motorhome.

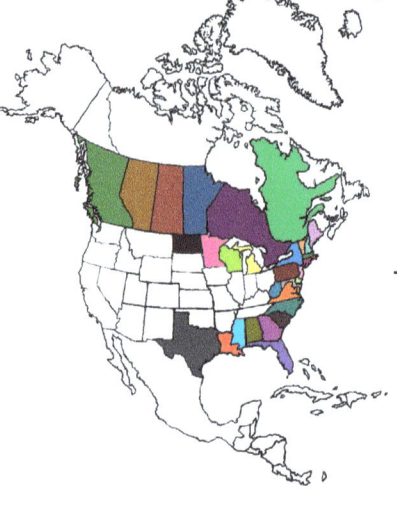

East Coast Dream Trip

To keep in touch with family and friends is my promise to myself. We've really kept very busy these past summer months visiting friends and relatives along the way and now we are beginning this newsletter of our "Dream Trip" to the East Coast.

Two months since we left home, and though we've been in touch by telephone, we haven't sent a single postcard yet. We really had to rush our Alberta visits because we had stayed in Vancouver long enough to acquire two future daughters-in-law, and was that ever an exciting way to begin our trip! Lots of new things to look forward to! From Chilliwack it was to Olds and Buffalo Lake in Alberta for more Herle family visits and fun!

August 16 was a celebration for my brother Stan and his wife's twenty-fifth anniversary in Edmonton, and they also will have two daughters-in-law in 1993. There is a nephew in Alberta and still another in Richmond, BC, who are also engaged, so it's going to be another good year!

After a visit to Marwayne, Alberta, to see a former construction friend of John's from thirty-something years ago, we entered Saskatchewan to see John's cousins. They drove us to the Denzil area where John's family and grandparents once lived. There was so little that was familiar to him—the big hills he remembered were just mounds now, the big creeks dried up and farmed over, and only a few buildings in his hometown were recognizable.

John at his old schoolhouse.

One of our "Coast to Coast Campgrounds" (CCC) is in Winnipeg, where a casual conversation with a fellow camper resulted in our learning that this apparent stranger was actually a nursing friend of ours that we hadn't seen in more than thirty-two years! We'd kept in touch every Christmas since my student nursing days and we were on our way to find a phone to call them when they started up a conversation by looking at our bus and saying, "Couldn't find anything smaller, could you?" Later she admitted they'd made fun of us as they watched when we rolled in with our huge 40-foot bus and got settled, then John pulled out the front folding step. She said they commented on the "poor fellow who had to pull out his own step—it wasn't even electric like their new 5th-wheel trailer was." We told them we were so happy to connect with them so easily, then Diane said her husband "would talk to anyone, even to a fence post if it moved."

It just so happened that Art and Diane also belonged to CCC and when the bus from BC rolled in, she remembered that in our Christmas cards for the last two years, we had included our news of retiring and travelling in our bus conversion. So she took a wild guess when they saw us drive in, and that's how easily we met after all those years! She invited us to their place for her crock pot stew and a great visit.

Our bus is an MCI, manufactured in Winnipeg, so we hoped to see that factory but it was the weekend, and we had miles to make. We knew that the outer shells, or "skins," were made in Canada, then they were shipped south across the border to Pembina, North Dakota, to be set on the chassis that are assembled in the US. So, we too left Canada and entered North Dakota to stop in Pembina at the MCI bus assembly plant, where *Dragonfly* would have been born so many years before! We were most warmly greeted and treated to a personal guided tour of the plant and wow, you sure needed more than the smell of money to buy a new one! Definitely not within our means to have a newer one, but what a treat to see the inner parts before it would be a completed bus.

Minnesota was our next stop to see friends we'd met a few years before in Desert Hot Springs, California. Now we learned about corn and soybean crops, rather different from the grain and canola farms we'd known on the prairies. A big lesson for us is when we look at the maps—Saskatchewan, Manitoba, and Minnesota all sure do have a lot of lakes. We were now getting into rolling hills with lots of bush. John is very observant of the land and often comments like "this sure is good/poor farming country," "look at the crops, they are so short/tall here," or "this is great farming/

ranching country." His comments made me much more aware of our surroundings.

We saw all five of the Great Lakes, crossed Wisconsin, Upper Michigan, then the five-mile-long bridge over the Straits of Mackinac to Lower Michigan. Lake Michigan is on one side and the other is Lake Huron. We've sure learned a lot of geography. I had heard John mention the Straits of Mackinac before, when he told me that when he was only nineteen, he ordered a new truck from Windsor and sat for four days on a Greyhound bus to visit an Aunt Monica in Montréal before picking up his truck and driving it home to Alberta! What an astounding adventure for him! Remember? I said before that he was an amazingly extraordinary man and that's just another reason why.

We came back to Canada at Sarnia, Ontario, and visited the Marchands, former neighbours from Marine Drive in Burnaby, at their home in Chatham before continuing on to visit a cousin in Windsor. From there, we travelled on Lake Erie's edge to Niagara Falls. We rode on the *Maid of the Mist* towards the Horseshoe Falls. We donned the blue raincoats we were given, and soon discovered why the boat was called the *Maid of the Mist* as the mist in the air was so thick. I kept telling John that they could quit going so close—we are close enough. Our boat was thumping and vibrating from pushing against the current, the thunder of the falls was deafening, but the captain of the boat got us all safely, threateningly close to the majestic falls and back.

That is one awesome, wondrous place to see! We had to choose between seeing Ottawa or Niagara Falls. We certainly think we made the right choice. While there, we figured that if you go to Niagara and don't take the *Maid of the Mist*, it's like going to a banquet and not having the main course or dessert. It's that special. We paid the fee and most certainly felt that we got our money's worth.

Navigating our huge bus among the traffic on the QEW [Queen Elizabeth Way] through the Toronto area with ten and twelve lanes of traffic was really something we won't miss if we never do that again! We made it to Montréal before the Labour Day weekend traffic began, and were happy grandparents again for a whole month! Karen, Serge, and Marc took us to a county fair in the Eastern Townships (just north of Vermont). Great horses there, lots of cattle of all kinds, and all the fun things of a county fair. John especially liked the fancy well-groomed horses. Marc enjoyed the carousel rides.

Dragonfly was parked about twenty miles outside of Montréal at our friends' place, the Gravels. They are a special family that Allan did a student exchange with while in Grade 10. The Gravels wrote such a warm welcoming letter to him and made his visit a memorable one. Later, they came to stay with us for Expo 86. Nicole was bilingual and was kept very busy translating between our husbands who were not, and my French was so minimal as well. We had no idea how much our lives would be intertwined after that.

From their yard, we drove to Montréal to stay at Karen and Serge's home. Every weekday morning after they left for work, we'd pop Marc in the stroller and strut off to daycare to keep up his routine. During the day we did little housekeeping things and got to read the daily newspaper, which was a luxury for us. We'd pick up Marc early so he'd usually be home when his mommy and daddy got home from work. We did this for a week, and on the weekend the Gravels, Jacques and Nicole, asked us to go with them to the Gaspé for a week in our bus. There was another couple as well, and three of us spoke good English. You should have heard some of the French-English conversations we had! Very interesting!! Sometimes louder is easier to understand, and laughing and hand gestures always help.

One particularly memorable scene was after our friends had shopped for everything we needed for a picnic lunch. We drove to Bic Park, just south of Rimouski on the north shore of the Gaspé and we wanted to eat outside because it was such a beautiful day.

There being no picnic tables nearby, we raised a few eyebrows in the area when we raised a bay door and took out our own interlocking picnic table that my dad had made, and some lawn chairs, and had our picnic right there under some giant trees beside the parking area, above the shores of the incoming tides.

The Gravels with us; Nicole in the centre, her husband Jacques, and me at Bic Park.

We saw how the nets are placed for eel fishing. We visited Miguasha National Park where there are heavy fossil beds and we got to beach-comb and crack some of the soft slate and found some small fossils. We learned that at one time that area was actually tropical! Just across the river from there is Dalhousie, New Brunswick. We were delighted to see the very famous Percé Rock and waited for low tide so we could walk right out to it. We also saw a grounded Peruvian freighter that we now recognize in a local TV commercial. It wasn't lobster season, but we got fresh scallops, shrimp, cod, sole—and our friends made some lovely meals with them. Oh, it was all so fresh. My love of seafood was being satisfied.

Tourist season was closing already, and watching the news we learned that the fish are so few now, many fishermen have to leave their boats and find other jobs to pay their rent. Listening to them, many Quebecois are just as fed up with the politicians and the referendum as we are. They don't want to leave Canada for their own sovereignty. They just want jobs and to be able to work. We also want Canada to stay whole, the way it is.

From there, we came back to Montréal for another two weeks of pure grandparenting pleasure. Walks through the park, crawling on the floor, playing in the sandbox, cuddling, clapping with Marc as he giggles and says "yay" and then bows. He's one-and-a-half tomorrow, has reddish hair—not much—has the sweetest smiles, and blue eyes and short legs. His little legs just churn when he runs.

John and Marc.

It was hard to leave Montréal in one way, and John had said we would stay until Marc says, "Grandpa," or when the leaves turned colour. We left when the leaves turned colour. Serge took us to the Laurentians for our first and only ever helicopter ride, to see the beautiful changing colours of fall. We'll just have to wait to hear Marc say "Grandpa" on the phone.

The fall colours of New England, in these first two weeks of October are at their peak. We came through Vermont to New Hampshire. Our campsite there was on the lake where *On Golden Pond* was filmed. You can take a boat ride to Thayer's Cottage and to Purgatory Cove and where old Walter the fish lived. We didn't splurge on the boat ride. Just took a snapshot at the lake. Lots of rolling hills around here and the splotches of colours are as nice as we have ever seen in any pictures.

Something we'd never seen before that is very common here in New Hampshire is that the house and garage or barn are all connected by building additions so that the result is a monstrously large building and they are all white so the fall leaves' colours now really help them to stand out, as well as the small white churches.

Two days ago, we drove into the White Mountains of New Hampshire by car on a slower road than the interstate we came in on, and went on a two-mile hike/climb along a huge chasm called the Flume that reminded us of the Maligne Canyon in Jasper. We learned that New Hampshire is the granite state and there are even granite curbs. They sure sparkle in the sun!

No major problems with the bus so far. Twice we returned from an outing to find water running out of the bay that has the tanks in. Both times a hose had burst, and John was able to repair it quickly, so no damage was done anywhere. We spun on some wet grass in the Gaspé one morning as we tried to climb up a slope out of our campsite and for a few minutes we were thinking "remorquage" or however you spell tow truck in French. But John backed up again and took a run from another angle and swerved his way out.

We've gone through rain and mud and construction. John has had to wash *Dragonfly* and the car many times. He's tried so often to organize "bus washing parties" but no one ever comes to them.

Other than a couple of colds and sneezing sessions, John's been doing very well. Me too. So, we've made it driving through and around Montréal, the QEW, and today the Maine turnpike, and we're still about 1,500 miles away from meeting my youngest brother Pat and his wife, Tammy, in Orlando in early November. So there's still lots to do. We have a 1-800 number for messages with our membership in the Family Motor Coach Association. This is invaluable as we can be only a phone call away from family, and pay phones are easily found on our routes. We are able to check for messages almost every day.

Co-piloting is such a continuous job because this is all new and unfamiliar territory to us. I don't even bring out my knitting because I'm too busy reading maps, guide books, and/or watching the road and exit signs. We have our reservations for Texas so our mail can go there now until the end of February. We'll spend March coming home for our son Al's wedding in April. We have sent our Donna, Texas, address to friends and family letting them know where we will be staying for December, January, February, so maybe this Christmas we can get some more mail from home. We were so happy to get over a hundred Christmas cards in Montréal last year. Just know we are making a long-awaited trip come true.

Our Moody Beach Campground at Wells, Maine, is just a few miles south of Kennebunkport and just north of the York-Ogunquit beach areas. Apparently we picked the most beautiful beach area of Maine, because north of Portland the coast is very rocky. So, we are now on the Atlantic!

This kind of travel feels like what cruising must be like, except we are cruising on land with no support staff. No room service or chefs, but constant changing scenery and discoveries. So, we declared today as a day off to catch up on some chores such as car washing, laundry, housecleaning, visiting, and relaxing.

We have really enjoyed Maine. Wow, the beaches on the south coast of Maine are gorgeous! They are SO clean in some areas, there's not a pebble or a shell—just packed sand. Lovely strolling. There's also "Marginal Way" a one-mile shoreline path along a rather rocky cliff area that was so beautiful we walked it twice and still had a long beach walk on the sand the same day. We toured that area for five days, had fresh lobster, lobster bisque, fresh haddock, and cod and clam chowders. We bought our first lobsters from a fisherman's wife who boiled them while we learned what to do with them when we got them home. We took a picture of them on our plates in the motorhome, and after that we got messy! I'm glad we weren't in public!! The second and third times we had lobster we were in a restaurant and felt more secure about digging out the meat.

Learning to eat lobster privately.

We have now skirted Boston and entertained thoughts of seeing the sights and history—the Freedom Trail, the Boston Tea Party, Paul Revere, etc.—but we cannot afford time nor money to do these extras, and the song about falling in love with "quaint little villages" in old Cape Cod kept going through my head, so we went to Cape Cod instead.

There certainly are quaint buildings and now we know more about Cape Cod architecture. And, we had no idea that Cape Cod is SAND and is eroding dangerously fast. The tip of Cape Cod will possibly be an island in the future because of the erosion! Hyannisport and the Kennedy summer homes are there too, and very impressive as was the Bush estate at Kennebunkport. They are both easy enough to see, but not to enter!!

Yesterday we toured a Pilgrim Village in Plymouth where the people dressed and spoke as supposedly they did in the 1600s—got lots of pictures. Then we toured the *Mayflower II* and saw the Plymouth Rock. Oh—where we are is cranberry country. Makes sense: pilgrims, turkeys, Thanksgiving, cranberries. There are cranberry bogs all around us and all around the Miles Standish National Forest that we drove through yesterday on our way to Plymouth. Nantucket Island is old and quaint and has lots of cranberry bogs, but not Martha's Vineyard. It's more clay and a more modern area.

The town of Sandwich where Sandwich cranberry glass is made is also nearby. There is so much history in this area, but we're only spending a few days here and we'd need two months to see all we want to.

So far, everywhere has its own special charm. We've enjoyed every stop so far. As we are travelling south, we're also still travelling with the fall colours. Last night on TV we heard (besides the presidential debate) that this is the best colour in ten years because there haven't been early frosts, wind, or rain storms that knock the leaves off the trees. Are we ever pleased to have been here for this display of exceptional colours.

Tomorrow we'll cross Rhode Island, Connecticut, and stay in New York one night, then on to Amish country in Lancaster, Pennsylvania. From there we'll also visit Gettysburg and Washington, DC, as we enter the Virginias and the Carolinas.

The referendum is over in Canada and it got the briefest mention on TV as an intro to the Blue Jays parade in Toronto. We sure don't get much Canadian news, but we are very happy our Canada stays as is.

We've toured a lot in Pennsylvania and learned a lot about the Amish, saw the single horse and buggies on the road, saw five mules pulling a disc, toured an Amish homestead, and ate shoofly pie. We were very pleased to have seen all of this after hearing about the Amish, but never been among them before.

The town of Hershey wasn't too far away, so we toured their chocolate factory and purchased some sweet souvenirs for munch times. In Hershey there is a Chocolate Avenue and the street lights are shaped like Hershey's kisses!! We saw them and got a postcard of them. Just a few short miles away from there was the Seltzer Smoked Bologna factory. They claim theirs is the only wood-smoke factory left. Apparently the others use liquid-smoke flavouring. Got enough smoked meat for several meals, too.

At Gettysburg, our knowledge of the Civil War increased. So many places that we have seen were just names in our memories and we really had no idea we would be seeing so many historic places for real! There are many more to come.

We have a sheet of plexiglass attached to the inside of the door of the bus where we have an outline of Canada and the US with a set of colourful stickers to put on as we visit each province and state. It's also a proud display when the door is open to show anyone where we have been so far. We have filled in from British

Columbia to Québec already, and some northeastern states. Now our goal is more of the east coast, then the south coast.

On our way into Pennsylvania, we took a little jog through New Jersey where we just happened to find cheaper fuel than what we had seen in New York. After we arrived in Lancaster, Pennsylvania, we drove to Delaware for car gas and had lunch to say we were in Delaware. From Pennsylvania, we drove through Maryland and West Virginia to get to Front Royal, Virginia, close to Washington, DC.

When we called our cousin Michelle there, her dad, Leon, from San Francisco was visiting, so we sort of kidnapped him and drove along the Shenandoah Valley's mountains on the very scenic Skyline Drive, and toured Washington, DC, by a trolley that let you off and on at your choice of stops. We parked at Arlington Cemetery and toured from there. That city is so packed with people and vehicles, it's a zoo there. We really lucked out by finding the visitor's centre (VC) when we did and followed their suggestion on taking the trolley. The third day with Leon, we toured the place of the Battle of Bull Run for more Civil War history lessons. We had such a lovely visit with him, enjoying him as a great tour guide and his wealth of knowledge of American history in that area for us.

By then we had learned that the location of Washington, DC, was a combination of the North and the South—a piece of land from Maryland to the North and a piece of land from Virginia for the Confederates. We have been very surprised to see the Confederate flag in some yards and even on some RVs in the parks. We heard one lady say there are some people still fighting that war.

Almost all October we've seen Halloween decorations on the homes we pass—corn stalks used extensively on gate posts or fences, scarecrows everywhere, pumpkins galore—as much decorations as some of us do for Christmas.

As we left Virginia to get here to North Carolina, we began to see our first cotton fields and some people and homes that certainly reminded us of some movies we've seen.

Dragonfly still turns a lot of heads. Whenever possible, we meet the other owners we see. There's a kinship among bus-conversion owners, maybe because we recognize the amount of work involved to do one. We expect to see many more as we get further south, but for now we're sort of the novelty in a campground and people will come over and say they saw us at another campsite or they watched us come in and have some questions about this. One nice gentleman said he was seventy-five and just had his first motorhome and he really wanted to know how people went about doing what we did. When we invited him in to see, he was delighted. Said he never expected to see the inside and, wow, would his wife ever like all this space!

We have been staying in our membership Coast to Coast Campgrounds [CCC] every night since we left Québec and expect to do so until we settle in Texas at a rented spot during "peak season." It's been an unbelievable $1 per night so far!! Definitely Coast to Coast was the right group for us to join.

Back to South Carolina. We have heard so much about Myrtle Beach so we were anxious to spend some time there too. Gorgeous beaches and miles and miles of fine white sand reminded us of what we saw in Cancun ten years ago. We strolled along these beaches, toured a plantation home, and saw some of the basket-weaving specialties of the area and watched some being made. I chose some small ones to buy for our girls at home. We are most certainly loving this warm weather.

Our second campground in South Carolina was at Yamassee and the lady at the registration centre directed us to our spot and explained the amenities, including the nature trail around Alligator Lake, and yes, there were alligators there! It sure didn't take us long to go on that nature trail and, be darned, we saw our first alligator in the wild and talked to people about them. Other newcomers had gone for bread and were feeding it to the gator so they could get him on their video camera!!

About then we learned that a gator can run fast enough on land to catch a person and some curious dogs, but they can't turn very fast, so if any of you are ever chased by an alligator, just run zigzag or turn instead of running in a straight direction!! You never know when that bit of information might come in handy—maybe never, and we don't plan on ever having to test that fact!! So far, the alligators we've seen are so well fed already that they don't want us.

In Florida, our first week was at Salt Springs before we toured St. Augustine on the coast, and Silver Springs, which was also a surprisingly great place. Silver Springs has natural springs that are so clear that this is the place where the glass bottom boat was first invented, or so we were told.

The huge springs feed a river that flows to the ocean with 99 percent pure water. (The rest is 'gatorade.) Many Tarzan movies have been filmed there as well as some more recent movies that involved statues on the bottom of the ocean floor. It was so beautiful to see such clean water—right down to where you could see the churning of boiling water coming up from the ground. We were taken on a jeep safari and saw lots of beautiful animals and lots more alligators. Our jeep driver with her blonde, curly hair reminded us of our niece Becky Vilcsak.

There sure are a lot of long-needled pine trees all the way down from Massachusetts and still here in Alabama. Lots of baskets to be made. There are also the live oak trees dripping with Spanish moss all along the coast here, too. The humidity is so high that sometimes, when it's hot, I feel like I'm in a bathroom where someone has just had a long hot shower and didn't use the fan or open a window. Very steamy. We've used the air conditioners a few times and sure do appreciate them.

We have managed a fax letter back and forth to Al, got the occasional greeting on our message service, and we're looking forward to having our mail soon in Texas. On the day we drove to St. Augustine, we drove back near Daytona Beach. We'd been seeing these roadside stands selling "Hot Boiled Peanuts" so we stopped at a citrus stand and, with our purchase of grapefruit and oranges, the lady gave us samples of hot boiled peanuts. They tasted like tinned kidney beans. I guess she could tell I didn't really like what was in my mouth. She said you have to acquire a taste for them. Yes, ma'am, you do. We also tasted fried peanuts. Salted, they were really good. This is peanut and pecan country, as well as citrus fruits.

Our CCC near Disney World was only about six miles from the main gate and we got there the same day as my brother, Pat, and his wife, Tammy, from Edmonton. We left a message at their hotel and had lots of time doing fun things together that week—they hardly recognized John who had grown a full beard and moustache since we left Québec over a month ago. It was the first and only time in his life to have all this facial hair, so he certainly did look different.

From Quebec to Florida, John grew a full beard.

We'd meet Pat and Tammy somewhere everyday and even managed a couple of quiet BBQ evenings at our "house." Doing the touristy thing in Disney is very expensive, we discovered, but it was a great place to see. Epcot Center is fantastic. We had a lot of fun at MGM studios too. The 3-D Muppet movie was so great we saw it twice. At various scenes we were sprinkled, had bubbles in the theatre, smelled citrus, marsh, seaside, or smoke, when it fit into the show. Saw a play of *Beauty and the Beast* and saw the set for *Honey, I Shrunk the Kids*, and *Roger Rabbit* (John proudly posed beside Jessica Rabbit). We also saw the tool belt from *Home Improvement* (Karen and Serge got us hooked on that show), even an Indiana Jones stunt show. We somehow got cast as Mr. and Mrs. McDowell, the neighbours in *The Golden Girls* in a segment on stage (not to be shown outside the MGM studios). Our autographs are still free!!

And, the *Teenage Mutant Ninja Turtle*s came in their pizza-mobile, did a little show with April O'Neil and then they stood around for autographs. We sure hope our pictures turn out, especially for our nephews, Danny Perka and Bradley Herle.

That was as far south as we went in Florida, and we will have some very lovely memories of that week. We avoided going any further south because of the recent massive devastation of Hurricane Andrew.

Instead, we went north in Florida to Live Oak, which was close enough to Georgia to go back there by car so we could spend a day at the Okefenokee Swamp. What an unusual sight! Cypress trees growing in the water—it was too cool for the alligators to be out sunning that day, so we saw only a little one on the swamp boat ride. Our guide said that one was probably just born in May of this year.

There were two other outstanding things in that campground. One was that they had a baby sinkhole—one that was very new. We walked into the bush to see it—maybe eighty feet across and forty feet deep. The ground just sank in, with all the trees and grass just fallen in, bare dirt sides, and it was beginning to collect water. We learned that Florida has lots of sinkholes and they are very unpredictable. We'd seen that on TV long ago but never thought about us actually ever seeing one.

The other interesting thing was this was the "Spirit of the Suwanee Campground," specializing in country and gospel music weekends. The Stephen Foster Memorial Park was there because he made the Suwanee River so famous when he wrote *Old Folks at Home*. There happened to be a Frontier Days special at the Stephen Foster Museum Park, where we were able to see lye soap being made, home preserves being done, old farming and cotton growing machinery, and lots of bus loads of excited, noisy kids running all over the place.

Sure is funny to learn new names of stores to look for to buy groceries. In Myrtle Beach, we got groceries at a Harris Teeter and just bought some money orders at a Tom Thumb (like a 7-11) at a Citgo service station. For fresh meat and produce, we were directed to the local Piggly Wiggly. I thought *Designing Women* made up that name!

We hadn't realized that Florida's northern panhandle is so long. Our third place in that state was north of Pensacola at Milton, near Alabama.

We discovered the gorgeous narrow strands of sandy beaches that form the barrier islands, a system that separates the mainland from the Gulf of Mexico, protecting the shores of the mainland. Navarre Beach was there, part of the many, many miles of sand, small dunes, and sea oats. It was almost deserted but for a few people fishing on the pier and a few others in wet suits doing some surfing.

We chose a short drive of only about a hundred miles to the next campground, which was in Alabama, so we could be near enough for sightseeing by car in the Mobile area. Back at the campground, there was a movie scheduled that night. It was *Sister Act* and you're right, sister Lucy, it sure is funny!

In Mobile, we toured the *USS Alabama*, an enormous battleship. It seemed like we were climbing up and down ladders and crawling through round doorways between compartments for hours. Wow, it must have been crowded when it was in service. There were bunks strung up in every available space. We also explored a submarine, a B-52, choppers, and bombers of all kinds in the enormous Battleship Park.

Driving along these beautiful barrier islands, we see that these homes are built on stilts maybe fifteen feet high, with plenty of room for the car and the boat to be parked underneath. These barriers are a string of islands from Florida to Louisiana, sometimes just strands of sand three or four hundred feet across—not very wide. We learned that preservation efforts are made to prohibit or limit foot traffic along the beaches by building boardwalks for beach access paths so the little plants and sea oats have a chance to take root and slow the erosion.

One naturalist we talked to said there is quite a controversy about insurance claims for people who insist on building on such fragile areas and he wonders why people are even allowed to build on these areas in the first place, when they are probably not more than five feet above sea level, and are so subject to the storms and possibilities of hurricanes. Seems like taking the chance of disaster is worth it to many so they can have a waterfront home for relief from heat in the summer. It's really quite deserted at this time of the year, but the temps are still in the 70s Fahrenheit or 20s Celsius, so I would think this could be a nice place year round.

We decided to drive right through Mississippi and settle the bus in Louisiana and backtrack by car to do our Mississippi and Louisiana sightseeing from here. The threat of the Pierce County tornadoes, 45 of them, are currently north and west of us. We hear all these weather reports that sound very serious, and there is an eerie stillness in the tall skinny trees around us. We are concerned but nobody around us seems worried so we won't worry either. In less than twenty-four hours the next storm will be gone and we will be free to drive in sunshine again. We are safe. If we had to, we could just drive away, but we listen to radio and TV reports, and for us, right now, all is well.

Looks like we'll be here in Louisiana for American Thanksgiving, and we expect to be in Donna, Texas, by the first weekend in December. Boy, it's been cold—close to freezing. And, it's the end of the American Thanksgiving weekend. Today everyone will be returning home and the roads will be jammed so we'll sit around here between New Orleans and Baton Rouge for one more day. We're not doing near the driving around here that we planned because we forgot about it being a holiday weekend and because it's COLD.

The day before Thanksgiving we drove into New Orleans, about 50 miles south of us. The first magnificent thing we saw was this long bridge we were about to cross, over Lake Pontchartrain into New Orleans. It's twenty-four miles long! Honestly! We can show you the postcard!! It's almost a half hour of driving across the water. What an extraordinary experience for us, we love this travel life.

We found the French Quarter in New Orleans, parked and walked around. Saw the fancy, ornate, lacy designs in the wrought-iron railings and balconies. They are absolutely as gorgeous as any photos we have ever seen. And here we are, walking among them! Us! We chose a funky little restaurant to try a bowl of gumbo for lunch. John's seafood and okra was tastier than my chicken and sausage, and if there will be a chance, we'll certainly try more gumbo bowls later.

We saw such an interesting slide presentation given by the National Park Service of the above-ground cemeteries in the area. Because of the high-water table on this marshy bayou area, they learned the hard way that you can't keep a coffin down when there are heavy rains, and there are heavy rains every year!

We strolled along a boardwalk on the banks of the Mississippi River and listened to a steam calliope being played on the Steamboat Natchez, docked very nearby. The calliope music was pretty strong competition for some nearby street musicians beginning their day—this was mid-afternoon and I guess the joint really gets hopping at night, but this afternoon we found Café du Monde and tasted the famous beignets, just as every tourist there should do. Unless we were with a tour, we chose to heed advice and not stay by ourselves at night. Pre-Thanksgiving festivities were beginning and the Superdome would be having big football games on the weekend and that's not our kind of wild party. We're safer in the campground.

To celebrate Thanksgiving Day, the park was providing the turkey and gravy, the rest was from the campers. I signed up to make a bread stuffing and my three-quart casserole dish had only about two tablespoons of stuffing left in it after dinner, so I guess it was well received. We met a Calgary couple who are in their sixth year of full-timing. It's still not at all a common thing for Canadians to do.

Then the weather turned even colder. It's really nippy now. No frost yet, but so close. Also met a couple from Pennsylvania in a school-bus conversion that reminded us of the Clampetts in the TV show *The Beverly Hillbillies*. I'm sure they were as proud of it as we were of ours.

Spent a few hours wrapping Christmas gifts—had just purchased the gift wrap when we shopped for Thanksgiving, but decided instead to use what I did for wrapping (the comics pages). Makes for some different reading material before you throw it away. Now I still have these rolls of Christmas wrap left … Sure felt good to get that box in the mail so early.

Yesterday there was popcorn stringing then tree decorating here in the campground, a gumbo supper, and Santa's visit. We chose instead to go into town and look around before the 4:00 p.m. Mass, then treated ourselves to a Cajun supper. John had catfish, I had bay snapper. Both were fillets stuffed with crawfish and other seafood. John's was really good, mine was also really good and spicy!!

Tomorrow night, November 30, we expect to be in Baytown, Texas, just east of Houston. Next will be Corpus Christi, then to our new home—Donna, Texas!! I see we will still be about 240 miles south of San Antonio then, and the nearby airports will be at McAllen, Harlingen, and Brownsville. We know there are apartments to rent in our campground, besides space in our motorhome, so let's see who's coming to Texas to vacation this winter! We are able to keep in touch by phone with our kids and Mom and Dad, and send newsletters to keep us in touch with our mailing list.

Now we're parked at Baytown, Texas, settled on Galveston Bay. We drove 312 miles today—over many miles of bridges crossing swamps and bayous. Swaying pampas grass lined the median for miles along the highway at Lake Charles, Louisiana.

We were so warmly greeted by our campground host who invited us to a "catfish fry" that evening. It seems like winter visitors (not called snowbirds here) are so welcome in Texas. The community is competing to see which campground can send the most visitors to their free fish fry and welcome party. Did we ever luck out, not only with the wonderful welcome, but also the good food, lovely evening. They separated John and me so we'd meet others. I happened to be seated beside the editor of the local newspaper; John said he sat by the mayor. Huge differences in the warmth of greetings and welcome feelings from some places in Yuma that we've heard about.

While there, we met an elderly couple who were newlyweds and very interesting. He was a geologist who had gemstones in the Smithsonian, both people were very interesting. [We would meet Gerry and Alice a couple years later when we saw their names on a map of a campsite in the Yuma area, and shocked them by dropping by their place to say hello again. Still later, we met again when they settled in Arizona and we saw some of his precious rocks in their home. And that's how easy it is to make unforgettable friends that you may never see again, but can never forget.]

NASA's Space centre was another highlight of that area. The visitor areas were open that day but would be closed the next day because of the next shuttle going up. Only families would be allowed tomorrow, so we think we are so fortunate to see the room and the chairs where staff and families would be, the rooms we see on television when we watch the progress of a shuttle. It's kind of surreal, and I love it and am so grateful to be here.

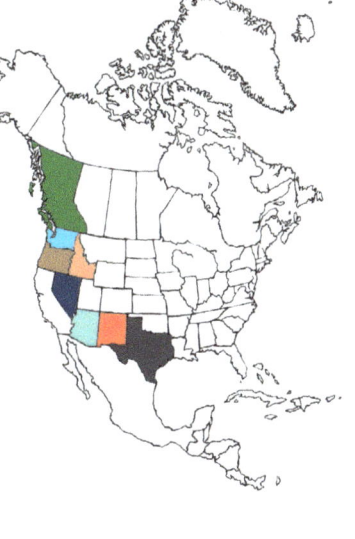

Texas, My Parents' Last Holiday

As soon as we arrived at our Texas winter home, John decided to shave so as not to confuse new friends. He found good friends in the pool room and learned to play horseshoes. I joined in quilting, crafts, and pool exercises. We both loved the music and dancing.

We loved the Rio Grande Valley in Texas for those three months—long enough to have a phone, a petunia patch that seemed to feed some local bunnies, and make more very dear friends. Our Surrey bus friends, the Gleadles, were there also, and there were so many activities we shared with them, yet we all had different interests as well.

It seems that snowbirds migrate rather directly south. Here in Texas, there are many Manitobans. In Florida, most are from Eastern Canada. British Columbians, Albertans, and Saskatchewanians go mainly to California and Arizona. I just hadn't considered that before.

During our stay there, a new friend, Millie, and I chose to tutor two Grade 4 students for a while with the HOSTS program (Help One Student To Succeed) at a local elementary school. We were told that we may be the only non-Hispanics these children might know, and that they have to qualify to join the groups. There was a huge map at the front of the class where the volunteers such as us put a pin in the map to show the students where we call home. There were a lot of scattered pins on that map.

The students were so shy and eager to learn. Together we would read a story, then ask questions. If the student could answer, we knew they understood. If some words were not understood, they were listed for the teacher as terms to give more help with.

We both thought we'd do this again if we could. At the end of one session, Millie was very sad. She said she had to say goodbye to one of her students because it was time for his family of migrant and seasonal workers to go further north. She said her student did not want to move away.

At the end of the program, there was a special evening to thank the volunteers. It was so interesting to know that the volunteers were not just winter visitors; we were among local firemen, police-men, and former students of the HOST program who were giving back to their community. Oh, we felt so richly rewarded ourselves. Each of us was given a laminated placemat with a photo of us with our student. How precious! (Years later, I would have an opportunity to join this program again in Yuma.) I felt so rewarded to be able to give back to the community that was welcoming and letting us enjoy its warm weather.

My Mom and Dad came to Texas in late February to join us to see the countryside for 1,200 miles from Donna, Texas, to their winter home in Apache Junction, Arizona, just outside the

Phoenix area. We had invited them for either a two-week stay with us in Texas, or to come with us as we travelled home. They chose to come when we would be driving home so they, too, could see more new countryside.

While Mom and Dad were there, we learned that we had suddenly lost a young nephew. We needed to speak to John's sister but had no idea how or what to say, so I asked Mom and Dad to please just go for a walk so we could talk on our own. Our families are close, and we hadn't dealt with anything like this while being so far away. We knew when we started this lifestyle that we may have times like this but when it happens, it's a shock. Still, we had to deal with it. We were so glad to have made that call, to let them know we love them and are hurting with them, even if we would not be there in Alberta with them for months yet.

By the time we left Texas, we had arranged with Jack and Muriel and two other couples that we'd travel the Baja together next winter. But life changes.

John, me, mom, Muriel and Jack Gleadle, our friends from Surrey who were in Texas with us.

As we drove on our road home with my parents, we visited the Alamo in San Antonio, and rode a boat alongside the famous Riverwalk area of the San Antonio River. Some people make a quick lasting impression on you, and one of them was our boat driver, who introduced himself as Fast Eddie. He made the river trip so interesting and funny that I think there couldn't have been a better entertainer for us on that day.

From there, we drove to see the colourful, sometimes very narrow passages of the Sonora Caverns, with lighting showing the delicate translucent stalactites and stalagmites.

In New Mexico, the huge cavernous Carlsbad Caverns—though gigantic compared to the Sonora Caverns—were shades of monochromatic browns. We wore headsets, listening to commentary as we walked along the marked trails, seeing the awesome football-field-sized spaces—or, at least, they looked that big to me. What a surprise for all of us when we learned how far we had walked underground and that Mom and Dad had walked one and a half miles of underground paths!

While we were driving the next day, my mom was sitting on the sofa and braiding coat hangers as she enjoyed the scenery, when she suddenly called out "javelinas"! I had never heard of them being around there and had no idea how she knew what they were (she couldn't explain it either), but she saw them running in a field and recognized them. In another area, we learned that they were indeed present, rummaging at the bases of some of the nut trees, damaging trees and crops and being a real nuisance.

We drove across New Mexico to a destination in Tombstone, Arizona, where we could see Boot Hill Cemetery, saloons with "bird cages" on the upper rows, and many Western-themed sights that John enjoyed so much, like the place where the shootout at the O.K. Corral took place. John loved his Western books and movies, and now he was seeing their real settings. I won't forget seeing the world's largest rosebush, which arrived so many years ago from

Scotland as a cutting for the homesick Scottish wife of a silver miner in Tombstone so she could enjoy roses from her homeland.

For a couple of days, we stayed in a campground on the grounds of nearby St. David's Monastery where we, very surprisingly, met some relatives of John's sister Hilda and her husband Denis! When the campground host saw we were from British Columbia, Canada, she said, "Oh, we have some others here from BC, maybe you'll know them." Hah! What were the chances? One in a million? Yes, it was a brother of Denis Wunderlich, husband to John's sister Hilda!

We visited in Tucson with cousins before returning Mom and Dad to their place in Apache Junction. From there, John and I took a new road home through Las Vegas, Reno, Bend, and, too soon, saw snow on our way.

A little side story about these cousins from Tucson, John and Esther Feldman. While we still lived in Burnaby, we got a phone call one day from my John's relative, Ursula, asking us to come to meet another relative. Turned out to be a long-lost cousin to the Herles. My John had always wondered where John Feldman went after he was orphaned in Saskatchewan in the 1930s. The two Johns finally met and asked so many questions about each other. John F. went east as a young man, married, had a family, moved to Tucson, built up a manufacturing business, and never knew that he had a score of relatives! When John F. asked my John about himself, he asked who John H. had married, since both guys came from the same town in Saskatchewan. When he learned that John H. had married me, he asked who my parents were. They were Stan and Rose Perka. Who was Rose Perka? She was a Keller from the Provost, Alberta, area. Now, the total surprise … My mom had looked after John F. when he was very young. Her youngest brother was John F.'s best friend at the time, my uncle, Tony Keller!

John F. remembered that the Keller household was always so happy and filled with music. Also, my dad, Stan Perka, was John

F.'s teacher and remembered him as a very good student and baseball player. How simply uncomplicated this small world is! John and Esther discovered so much new family they never could have imagined. We visited them each winter, and on this trip again, when they got to see John F's childhood neighbour and also his school teacher—my parents. Each time they met after reconnecting was exciting for all of us.

Life takes some very quick turns, and we were about to take several more in the next year. We were home in the Vancouver area just in time to attend some bridal showers for our Allan and his fiancée, Jenny, and their wedding in April was so beautiful!

In May, our Karen got her requested transfer from Montréal to Vancouver, and she and Marc now lived in Vancouver. Marc was now two and a half and loved "Dampa's bus," and our brag book consisted of a few albums! Karen was still working with Revenue Canada, now in downtown Vancouver, as a single mom. Marc went to a French daycare so he'd be able to speak French to his papa and grand-mère and grand-père in Montréal.

In June, with Karen and Marc moved and settled, we went to a wedding in Edmonton and stayed for a Round Hill reunion in July, the area where I grew up on the farm. Mom and Dad and Marc rode with us in the bus to Edmonton, and then Mom and Dad came back with us later in July. Such freedoms we have when our bed is with us all the time.

Then the bridal showers began for our Keith and his fiancé Sandy's wedding in August. Another exciting session of showers, decorating parties, and planning for that very special day on August 21. Karen was an usherette and Marc helped her to lead some guests down the aisle in his little navy polka-dot bow-tie made by Sandy to match the bridesmaids' dresses. Marc looked so cute in his white shirt and navy pants, even if the white shirt was out of the pants even before the ceremony!

In September, we went by car with my brother Ken to Edmonton to help with some house building for our brother Dennis. It may take a while for Ken to remove the waltz and polka music from his mind, but John loved it! In October, all was peaceful and we got a lot of work done on the bus in preparation for our trip to the Baja. But this was not to be.

Dad wasn't feeling so good in the fall. This led to surgery on October 20 and we learned there was so much cancer throughout his abdomen that there was no way to remove it and palliative chemotherapy was offered. Mom was also feeling tired that summer and fall, and went through more tests and appointments to see why. She had a bone marrow test to go through in the very near future. So, they had a struggle ahead, as we all did as their family. There was no trip to the Baja—for now.

DECEMBER 1993
APACHE JUNCTION, ARIZONA

Dear family and friends,

Because John and I are the retired ones, we got to come here to a sunny, happy place to do a job we'd rather not need to do.

It's such a beautiful sunny day here again and today I went into the swimming pool for water exercises. I enjoyed the water so much that I told myself that I wasn't too smart for letting so many days go by without at least going for a swim. But we didn't come here for a holiday, and we don't have the same carefree enthusiasm right now. We're here to pack up my mom's and dad's personal belongings, sell the rest in a garage sale, and try to also sell their Park Model trailer here in Rock Shadows, Apache Junction, where they've spent the past five winters. They had full intentions of being here themselves, and our winter was going to be on the

Baja Peninsula of Mexico, in the Cabo San Lucas area. All that has changed.

So, now we're packing plywood-cutout sheets, depicting the Nativity scene that Dad made here last winter, into my brother Ken's van for the trip home to BC. Like Ken said before we left, "At least my van goes to Arizona, even if I can't!"

The neighbours in this park have been super to us. The outside of the trailer had been washed and the patio had been swept, and it all sparkled to greet us when we arrived. They visited and worked and cooked for us, just like family.

We call Mom and Dad every evening and ask questions and tell them what's new here. The Alberta family has been visiting them since we left, and all the new cooks in Mom's kitchen are helping keep up Mom's and Dad's appetites. So, that's our year past.

Two beautiful weddings and two beautiful daughters-in-law, along with having Karen and Marc so close to us, are the main events of the year. And, since October 20, we share the struggle to help Mom and Dad conquer what they can, and live with what they must. Remembering and reliving our good times should help us get through these bad times.

I had to laugh at John today when he told Uncle George that I acted just like a man this morning because I read the newspaper while he made the toast for breakfast!

January 1994. Our trip home was through some unpleasant weather, but uneventful. At least for us. Unfortunately, when we called home, we were told that our car had been in an accident when our sister-in-law was driving and was hit by someone not paying attention. Our car was totalled and dear Jo-Anne had a very painful shoulder injury. The reason she was driving our car was because we had borrowed their van to take to Arizona so we could haul Mom's and Dad's belongings all in one load. And we were not looking forward to telling them about a rock chip on their windshield!

John did all the insurance appointments and car shopping by himself because, by this time, we were spending a lot of time with Dad, taking him to the hospital for a week of daily palliative chemotherapy injections. The last injection would have been Christmas Eve but the hospital and doctor said Dad could have that day off.

By January, we had a grey Saturn car and Dad's chemo was on again for a week. Now we were taking him into hospital with a wheelchair and also sleeping at their house, only coming back to the bus to check on it or to sleep whenever a brother or sister from Alberta came to stay with Mom and Dad.

In February, Dad did his week of chemo but decided no more. The doctors agreed with him, and his condition has continued to deteriorate. However, the night before Dad's February chemo started, Mom's condition had become much worse. She ended up in emergency surgery for a perforated bowel on February 13.

So, every morning after Dad's chemo session we would wheel him up to see Mom before we went back to the house.

We knew Dad's cancer was terminal, and my brother Hilary had gone out with him to the funeral home a few weeks before, as he wanted to plan some final arrangements. At the same time as all this was going on with Dad, we learned that Mom's ongoing and long-term fatigue was due to what was now diagnosed as lymphoma. We were told that Mom's lymphoma would respond well to chemotherapy as soon as she was strong enough to begin treatment.

In March, we needed outside help besides the home care nurses who were keeping tabs on Dad and his pain control, so we began getting home support workers for two hours a day. Mom and Dad got personal care, and we got a bit of house help and were taught some handy hints for lifting and managing a wheelchair in the house.

Those home support care workers were angels without wings. One morning, I heard the sweetest words from one of them who was on the early shift. I was just up and came to the kitchen as one of the home support staff walked in from my parents' room. She said something like: "Both your parents had their morning bath, the bed is fresh, laundry is being done, and the coffee is on!" Oh, sweet, sweet words!

By this time we needed someone alert twenty-four hours a day for both Mom and Dad, though there were times during the day when Mom abandoned her walker and seemed to be making slow progress.

We'd had our laughs and we'd had our cries and we'd kept in touch with very few friends because it seemed there weren't enough hours in a day after the necessities and daily updates with the families.

From here, my thoughts may be incomplete but the day came when Dad and Mom made the decision together that it was time for Dad to go to palliative care as suggested during a doctor's visit. By the time the transfer was made the following morning, Dad was slipping away and was in hospital for just over a day. Mom worried that she would be too weak to attend Dad's funeral, but two days later she was hospitalized and scans found that her cancer was everywhere and she never had a chance either.

Mom's funeral was two weeks after Dad's. They were on April 7 and April 21, just before their next birthdays. Dad would have been eighty and Mom seventy-five; both birthdays not quite reached. Family came from Alberta for Dad's funeral and hardly had time to unpack after leaving before coming back for Mom's. Honestly, as we had to prepare for Mom's funeral, it felt like Dad's was a dress rehearsal or practice. I sure didn't like that feeling. Dad belonged to the Knights of Columbus and had an impressive honour guard at his funeral.

Our family was hurting so much, and because Mom's name was Rose, we decided to buy a bunch of red roses and hand them out to the ladies for as long as they lasted. Mom belonged to the Catholic Women's League (CWL) and the ladies lined the aisles, wearing blue jackets and white blouses, and each carrying a candle and a rose. Those are beautiful images in my mind.

I had been a CWL member at our St. Monica's Parish in Richmond when the kids were toddlers, but life got in the way and I hadn't been an active member for years. But after Mom's funeral, I wanted to be a CWL member again and have an honour guard like that at my funeral. (In the meantime, I can attend other members' funerals and be an honour guard for them, as I continue to do.)

My siblings and the spouses all worked together to empty the house and divide all that was in it, as Dad and Mom requested. It was quite a task, but there were nine of us and our spouses to share the work.

Because our space in the bus was so limited, we chose to keep only small items from their house. Still, John and I filled a small storage locker of memorabilia, and *Dragonfly* was checked out and rolled away as far as Chilliwack for the beginning of another adventure.

So, when you have the time to read on, let me share our next trip with you. We want to thank each of you who was a part of this trip, whether in a visit, by phone calls, letters you sent ahead to us, or the good example you've set for us.

We have a mission for this next trip: to go to sell Karen's home in Montréal.

The Road to Newfoundland and Back

Some sprinkles and some sunshine as we travelled from sea level to 4,400 feet in about two hours of leaving Chilliwack on May 13, 1994.

Last year, John had concerns about the bus power at times. It just didn't seem to keep its speed. At one point we saw an elevation sign and realized we'd really been climbing without being aware, so an altimeter is now mounted on the dash, as well as a compass, and we are much more aware of our altitudes and twisty roads.

We played our German polka and waltz tapes as we passed through the mountains. My dear brother Ken will remember them from last September, on our car trip to Edmonton. That sure wasn't Ken's favourite music, but John loves it, and Ken cared enough for him too, so John could have his favourite driving and dancing music on that trip

The vase of fresh carnations is still looking lovely, riding on the dash of the bus with a sympathy note from cousin Sharon Horner after losing both my parents. There were just a few snowflakes on Roger's Pass, more snow showers near Banff. Saw deer, elk, mountain sheep, and a bear. Very surprised to hear a Calgary radio station predict a low of 3 degrees Celsius tonight. Vancouver was so summery when we left! Some threatening dark clouds but, hey, any time someone wants rain and/or miserable weather around, just have us over for a visit. We settled onto our comfy cement parking pad at the Blatz home in Olds, Alberta, and quickly crawled into our bed because no one was home. It's Friday so Isabelle and Joe, John's sister and brother-in-law, would be out dancing. After 11 pm. there was this pounding on the bus and with shouts of "Get up! Get up!" so we got up to visit for a couple more hours. We were so tired!

We went into Calgary the next day to visit an Aunt Josephine in hospital, wanting to meet up with John's cousin Anne from the San Diego area, and his Aunt Monica from Montréal, who were meeting in Calgary this week. A chance remark by a nurse about the ladies staying on Motel Row nearby and us asking at a few motels there, finally got us to see and really surprise these girls by appearing at their door. There was cousin Anne Baronet, serving her homemade cookies from Vista, California, and Aunt Monica from Montréal, still another surprise when cousin Rose B. from Edmonton was there too. Such a surprised group we all were! The next two days were spent seeing John's siblings, Irene and her husband Ted, the Blatz families, and lots of nephews and nieces, and their families. Wonderful memories!

Tuesday, May 17, would have been my dad's eightieth birthday. We're heading into strong winds as we drive to Galahad where Frank and Doreen Herle had their son and daughter-in-law and granddaughters, as well as John's sisters, Ann Kuefler, and Lena Hauser and her husband Harold over for another very wonderful evening.

A very gracious welcome in Provost the next day included a parking spot right beside Uncle Mike and Aunty Elizabeth's home. It was a real treat to see cousins Tom and Katherine, to meet cousin Wally, and visit an old family friend, Gretchen, in the seniors' lodge.

The following day was mostly touring. We took time out to see where Dad taught school, where he met Mom, where they lived when the first four of us were born, and the quiet cemetery on Mount Carmel where their first-born premature twin boys were buried. We were driven by Uncle Mike through some very slippery and muddy roads that I would not have attempted, but then we'd have missed things like the old Eyehill School that Dad taught in. And when we went in, we saw a treasure trove of antiques and some junk.

I sat in an old school desk and tried to imagine Dad teaching there. There are textbooks stamped for Eyehill School, the outside bell is on the step, and the stove is still there too. Then to the Upland School site where Dad walked from Mom's family home where he boarded, and Mom cooked for him. Only a rock with a plaque remains to mark the spot, but Aunty Liz showed us where relatives like themselves and John F would have played ball in the schoolyard and where their homes were.

As we drove up the hill to Mount Carmel over a little-used road, we heard stories like the one about Dad giving Aunty Ceil and Mom a real "thrill ride" over those hills until he broke the springs in his car, or about Mom's first communion when the candle she was holding got too close to her veil and it caught fire and singed her hair, and about Uncle Tony's muddy entrance into the church for his first communion because their car got so stuck in the mud.

We saw the homestead where Mom grew up, and oh my gosh, the house looked small! I remembered it well when Mom's brother, my Uncle Adam, had his big family living there. And yet, somehow, there was room for us to visit and share meals.

Very hard to imagine the big family of twelve all fitting into it, but I do remember that we kids sat on the stairs with our plates on our knees at mealtime.

Uncle Mike spoke about the wonderful music those Keller boys could play, but during Lent the instruments were all put away. Then, oh! On Easter Sunday—the music and song they made!

Sometimes Mom's family went to another church, St. Donatus, built into a hillside. Aunty Elizabeth remembered when snakes seemed to be living in the church and would appear on the altar even during Mass! The church was built into the side of the hill and probably provided an excellent nesting area for snakes.

Next, to the Hauck family farm where we saw cousin Doreen and Andy, and some of their family, as well as some buildings still damaged by cyclones from years ago. Returning to Provost, we took a friend of the family, Gretchen, with us to the 5:00 p.m. Mass being said for Dad and Mom. Uncle Mike then barbecued some homegrown steaks, Tom and Katherine White joined us for another great evening. John and Uncle Mike challenged each other with yet another lively game of crib that evening.

Cold, rainy, almost the end of May—oooh it's wet and miserable! Said our good-byes and headed east; through Macklin where my mom and John were both born and through Denzil where the Herles lived. The road was not great. No towing lights working on the car! We pulled a boner with our electrical hookup in Provost because we weren't accustomed to the new wiring system, this being the first week the Saturn is being towed and it's different than the Honda was. No matter … John soon had the wiring fixed.

Quite flat around Kindersley going east to Rosetown. Suddenly we saw several cars at once. There had been no traffic and my first thought was "A funeral procession?" But … it's only been 6 weeks since Dad's and Mom's funerals. And, it was such a dull, gloomy day that everyone drove with their lights on anyway!

The trees are shorter in Alberta, they are just beginning to leaf out. In Vancouver, hay was already being cut when we left.

John calls a day like today a sleeping day but he's driving and I'm carrying on Mom's tradition of making covered coat hangers. No one needs to navigate today. The road is straight. The farmers are happy it's raining, but many fields are flooded from Kindersley to Rosetown. Saw one field only partially harvested—the combining equipment was sitting in the field in the rain. At Outlook we saw irrigation ditches and equipment. Such contrasts in weather conditions!

We did only pit stops, with lunch on the go. As we drove, we thought of our friends Joe and Marie Law, Harold and Carolle Hansen, accompanied by the tape we bought when we were all together at Fantasy Gardens in Richmond where we heard "The Chicken Yodel" being performed live.

Crossed the scenic Qu'Appelle Valley. Another name on my list of places to see. Now we know where Craven, Saskatchewan, is—the site of the big music festivals. Close to Regina. The Ring Road around Regina leads us to the campground we stayed in two years ago, and soon we were ready and gone to see cousin Jake and Mary Volk for a fun evening. After a scrumptious turkey dinner we saw Mary's looms and talents. Jake gave us a musical concert. We told Jake we thought we saw antelope, he said we'll see a lot more in Wyoming.

Heading east again, the crystal hummingbird given to us by John's sister Ann, finally had a chance to sparkle in the sun! After a few hours of driving, John, feeling very sleepy, decided to pull off onto a service road that had run alongside us for many miles. As is our luck occasionally, the service road suddenly ended there, as we turned directly onto a no-exit road!!!!!!! By the time we unhooked the car, backed up the bus to turn it around, and hooked up the car again, John wasn't sleepy any more, so we carried on.

We arrived east of Winnipeg via the wonderful Perimeter Road and settled into the CCC member campground. We called Art and Diane over for a visit—they are the couple we met quite by accident in that same campground, after corresponding with Diane for over thirty-two years since nursing school. She and John knew each other from being in the same home town, Heisler, Alberta. [Where, many times in these later years, I have stopped on my road trips to buy some excellent homemade sausage. But I only have a cooler, so wherever I stop for the night, I need someone's freezer. And, if I should forget my precious cargo in that freezer, the deal is that it's my loss, their gain. I always remembered it, shared some, but never forgot to bring it with me again.]

Still in Winnipeg, a lazy Sunday morning—found an 11:00 a.m. Mass at St. Bernadette's. The young priest had a most interesting homily about languages for Pentecost Sunday. He explained that he had no talent for languages as some do and it was especially hard for him when he was in a parish with predominantly non-English speaking people. He spoke about language differences and said the Italians have way too many vowels—they really should give some to the Polish and Ukrainians who seem to have hardly any!!! So true.

And, another note about languages. A few days later, while resting, I heard an interview of a person who had been to Poland and watched *Wheel of Fortune* in Polish. Funny, the lady said; the contestant chose a Z and there were three of them! She also said that contestants hardly ever bought a vowel! Just confirms what the priest said. Also, the prizes given in Poland were such staples as flour or oil.

Before our dinner date with friends Jack and Ai-Heung, formerly from Vancouver, we had a quiet time. I cut John's hair outside in the sunshine while being watched by a mother killdeer on her nest. Yesterday we had seen four eggs in her nest, and she was letting us know that she was feeling very harassed by our presence. Earlier in the morning, we'd been told one egg hatched and during the haircut, tiny birds walked away from the nest as she tried to distract us. When she saw we were no threat, she called her babies back, tucked them all under her again and stayed as still as a rock. A few feathers ruffled underneath her periodically as her babies moved about.

We learned from Jack later that evening that though the killdeer eggs are laid at different times, once she sits on them to hatch, they hatch almost simultaneously so they can leave their vulnerable nest on the ground all together as a family. Sure enough, the next day the nest was empty and no other campers saw them leave or knew where the birds were.

Oh, yes, our campground offered only electricity because water and sewer lines were still frozen due to the lack of snow to insulate the ground. It's almost the end of May!

That evening with Ai-Heung and Jack was so pleasant. We were talked into staying another day to go sightseeing with Ai-Heung and their daughter, Laura.

It was a delightful tour of Winnipeg. We saw Portage and Main, toured the gorgeous Legislative Building and learned how the huge bison carving inside was put into place by sliding it over a flooded and frozen floor to protect the Tennessee marble floors. Lunch was dim sum in Chinatown before we joined the Victoria Day celebrations at The Forks, where the Red and the Assiniboine Rivers meet. The city is a haven for cyclists because it's so flat, but that also contributes to the areas along the Red River being flooded at times, like the year past. Very glad we stayed.

Back at the bus, we learned Jackie Onassis was buried at Arlington Cemetery beside JFK, where we saw the eternal flame in October 1992 with Leon Vieux. Also heard the Saskatoon area just had golf-ball-sized hail. Good thing we're not there! We had serious hail damage on our Honda years earlier when visiting cousin Ken Keller in Calgary. We had a courtesy car from the autobody shop, which we were scheduled to return just before a long weekend when we'd pick up our car. Well, all was just fine, and the young employee was so anxious to get the use of the courtesy car for the long weekend, but as our car was being backed out of the repair shop, it was hit by someone cruising down the back lane, tearing off our rear bumper—which meant we did not get our own car back, and totally wrecked the plans the young fellow had for his long weekend. I still feel sorry for that kid. He looked so crushed.

Now it's a new road to us as we continue east in the sun. We plan to travel the Canadian route right across Canada! The beautiful farmlands have become rocky with heavy growths of evergreens and leaf trees. Lots of creeks, streams, and lakes as we enter Ontario. Roadkill: one arm chair and one muffler. Really clean roads here. Lake of the Woods area is so very scenic! Little lakes and beautiful views from the highway. Like *On Golden Pond* areas. Kamikaze dragonflies against our windshield.

Now rocks are growing trees. Beautiful names—Sugar Bay, White Lily Lake, Dad's Lake, Mom's Lake, Baby's Lake. Lakes everywhere, with pretty rock and tree islands. Shorter trees. Have to look to the right and to the left because there's beauty on both sides. Soon it looked more like farmlands. Cloud formations rolling along, puffy, changing shape. Saw a dead young moose off the road, and a live one a little further on. Deer and moose caution signs everywhere. Noticing that each province has its own unique provincial markers ... in Saskatchewan the roadside litter barrels are replicas of grain elevators. In Manitoba, they are white balls called Orbit. Signs tell you to toss your litter into Orbit—five minutes, ten minutes ahead, or whatever. Manitoba's provincial highway signs have a buffalo on them. Ontario's have a crown.

The Orbit trash can.

Trans Canada Highway 1 becomes Highway 17, or the King's Highway, in Ontario. John suddenly noticed as we entered Thunder Bay that the leafy trees were just beginning to turn green.

After settling in a KOA, we drove the car to see the Terry Fox Monument and saw the Sleeping Giant rock in the HUGE Lake Superior. Legend says an old Indian was turned into stone because he told a White man about the wealth of the amethysts in the area.

Phoned friends and family from an outside phone booth again while the mosquitoes tried to have their way with me!

A sunny day again, but "fresh" outside. Highway signs indicate we are on the Lake Superior Circle Tour and from now on it's where Terry Fox ran. Amethyst and pulp are the industries here, with lots of amethyst shops—makes me want to do some lapidary work at some time in my life, before or after I write a book. Many hours of travel just to go along the north edge alone of Lake Superior. Rolling hills, rock in abundance. River and stream waters looking black. It's yellowish when falling over rock. Oh no, not pollution, we hope!

No tapes playing, just the CB on to see if there's much trucker conversation. Nothing noteworthy 'til a friendly voice called out "Motor coach, how would you like to trade vehicles?" I answered him, "For how long?" He said, "Just 'til I could see some country." I explained that's what we're doing now and during the conversation he welcomed us here and assured us we would find a lot of very friendly people in Halifax. Such nice truck drivers.

Here's where we saw a big black bear, a helicopter placing new power poles, and a truck-mounted driller down the road making a lot of dust trying to drill into this rock. Little Pic River is really brown, and we saw where it enters Lake Superior and causes about a mile of wide contrasting brown water before it blends into the blue of Lake Superior. Makes us really wonder about pollution from logging and mining. At the northeast corner of Lake Superior the leaf trees are still bare. With such a short growing season they can't get very big, I guess, and now they need all the strength they can muster just to push their leaves out.

Meanwhile, on the dash of the bus, the amaryllis bulb and herb pots are doing fine. The herbs are parsley, cilantro, chives, and basil. As long as we stay in Canada, we can keep them growing, adding to scrambled eggs and salads.

Lots of hills—as long as twelve kilometres with a six percent grade. We would have no trouble counting the other vehicles on the road—not many at all! Water levels look rather high everywhere. At Marathon, a ski-lift area looked interesting to stop and see, but it was a very brief visit. It was very cold out there! Passed Yellow Brick Road by a gold mine. The White River has black water! Bell Canada is doing a lot of fiber-optic upgrading in the area. John says it's like a day's job just waving to all the guys we see now. Traffic has really increased.

Rain starting again—irritating John. It sure messes the car with road spray. Pulled into a provincial park with no attendant that looked too lonely. Went to KOA in Sault Ste. Marie. Views of Lake Superior have shown how vast the lake is—hundreds of miles of horizon that's just water and sky. We have driven all day and still only came around the north side of the lake. Interesting signs: "Have a Superior time"; "We live in a Superior Community"; "Have a Superior Vacation."

Just relaxed at home. Woke up to a cool morning but no rain. Dash light shows NOT GENERATING when we're ready to go. Causing more than a little concern for John who's out there working, saying his litany of "goddammits" and that his morning is spoiled but we'll have to go anyway and just can't use lights. We can get it fixed further down the road. As we drove a bit, the warning light went out and stayed out, so we're in a better frame of mind. Getting away from the rocky, cold lakeshore. Land flattened again to greener farming country. Areas of big rock again nearing Sudbury and then oh! A huge nickel refinery building with big smoke stacks—GINORMOUS! The Big Nickel refinery building looks about a half mile long—unbelievable! The highway through

Sudbury sure was busy and the narrow, twisting city streets made driving an adventure. It was 2:30 pm. and the sharp turns—with and without steep hills—were a real challenge to some, like the school bus driver who we kept a safe distance behind because he seemed to need all of his lane and some of ours when we were side by side.

We were pleased to see a sign and construction indicating a bypass road is being built and, boy, they sure need it! We usually take the bypass roads or the "beltway" as Ross Perot called them, but Sudbury gets all the through traffic right down its twisted main street, Kingsway.

Rocks and lakes, tiny and as huge as Lake Nipissing, are very impressive. Lots of heavy bush areas, and even saw daffodils a couple times and tulips once—their spring is on the way! Decided to quit in Mattawa at about 5:00 pm. and found a lovely campsite—only 15-amp service and no sewer sites—but on the beautiful banks of the Mattawa River. It appears that across the river is Québec—looks like a comfortable resort area there too. Population about 2,500 here. Went for a drive in the evening to find a bank machine, and decided this was a very pretty place.

It's May 27 and a sunny day, but frost is still on the roof of the car this morning! No wonder the trees are so slow to leaf out! Heading to Ottawa to settle for a few days. Signs of water sports in abundance. Generator light, okay. The amaryllis flower and herb garden are growing well on the dash. I'm watching them grow for about six hours every day as we travel, and the amaryllis is about eight inches high already.

Getting change from $20 at each campground so far. No more CCC until Québec and Nova Scotia as long as we're in Canada. Getting 6-8 mpg. depending on hills and windy days. Following the Ottawa River now, Québec is just on the other side all the way. Pastoral scenes along the Ottawa River Valley. Looks so peaceful. At a hundred kilometres from Ottawa, the roads are suddenly perfect! There is a good throughway through Ottawa; we chose a campground just past Ottawa so we'd get a quick glimpse of the city as we'd drive through, and we'd be that much further east when we leave. We plan to stay here for a few days. Recreationland Campground, as a Good Sam member, is $18 a night. Nice place.

Did lots of laundry, baked Cornish hen, and made an Arizona newspaper recipe for stovepipe bread. Watched an exciting hockey game between NY and NJ. In double overtime, NY won, so they will play the Canucks for the Stanley Cup and we will become sports fans until the Stanley Cup is over. Made phone calls to the east and to the west.

Watched Girl Guides set up tents. It's really chilly—the forecast includes frost warning. Though today was sunny, yesterday here was cold, rain, hail. That explains the leftover snow we saw west of Ottawa. Mosquitoes aplenty and they won't take "no" for an answer.

A cold morning. Studied the map and transit of Ottawa. Bread turned out not too bad. Miserable, cold, and rainy but at least we're not the Girl Guides tenting up the slope from us. Saw one girl wet her hairbrush under the outside tap and brush it through her hair! Almost made me shiver.

Decided to take the car into Ottawa, drove along Sussex Drive, over to Hull, Québec, to see the Museum of Civilization. Doesn't quite compare to Victoria, but it's a nice building. A wedding reception was being set up for about six hundred people. Ooh la la! Very pretty! Tried to take a picture of the table settings. Drove along the Rideau Canal near my nursing classmate's house. Will see her tomorrow. Drove back to Cumberland through the countryside, avoiding highways, and found a church for tomorrow morning. Home to eat and relax.

Sunday, sunny, and warmer. Went to 9:30 a.m. Mass at St. Marguerite Mary—last Sunday was Bernadette, my middle name, now Margaret Mary, my other names—when will we find a St.

John's? Decided to carry an umbrella into Ottawa as insurance. Today we visited Parliament Hill. At the tourist info we learned of FREE weekend parking at World Exchange Building on Metcalfe and Albert Streets. That's our price!

Parked the car there, booked a tour of the town on a red double-decker bus and saw a lot, including the governor general's residence, the prime minister's houses, the beautiful roads along the Rideau Canal, and also along the Ottawa River. An exceptionally warm day with a quick stop at the Central Experimental Farm, huge tulip beds beside Dow Lake, Hull, and then to the huge War Memorial. Walked to the tourist info tents, booked tours of the East Block and Centre Block. The East Block is offices, and we toured four restored rooms depicting the turn of the century. The Centre Block is our Parliament Building with the House of Commons and Senate.

We saw the immense library and posh Privy Council, entered by a long corridor, with coat hooks along the side. An interesting story about the coat hooks was that they were once assigned in order of the owner's importance. The prime minister's coat was nearest the door, and on down the ranks to the furthest hook from the door. When ranks were changed, the list of changes was given to a page, whose job it was to rearrange the new order of the coats on the hooks, according to the new positions. So, when the ministers came out from their meetings, they learned whether they'd been demoted or promoted if their coats were on different hooks. If their coat was on the floor, they'd been kicked out of cabinet! Such was the tact!

Our tour guide suggested that 2:15 pm. to 3:00 pm—Question Period at the House of Commons—is the most interesting time to visit. John said he'd also like to visit the Senate tomorrow to see how many Senators actually appear on the job! Saw the parliamentary grounds and the Centennial Flame there, then went to meet my nursing classmate Andrea and her husband Andy at 6:30 p.m.

We went to an Italian restaurant and talked and talked and talked—Andrea and I about a lot of things including our nursing days—John and Andy discovered they both worked on the same project in Cold Lake, Alberta in 1959! Back to see their new home, almost finished. Gorgeous!! Came home dead tired.

A dreary Monday. Decided to stay home and do some neglected paperwork. Did nineteen pieces of correspondence. Humid, a thunderstorm warning never materialized here. Mosquitoes are still ferocious. It was a good day to stay home. John read, I wrote. We were even able to arrange for a fax from brother Hil and Sandra. It sure is nice to keep in touch with the family.

A message from Keith sounded so happy when he told us he's NO LONGER A STUDENT! That boy was one who had to leave home because his parents sold the house! You've heard of mean parents like that? Well, not really that bad, I think. It was going to be a long road of studies to be a medical doctor, so he ended with a couple of degrees before his health inspector degree. He had lived away from home a couple of times. He took a year off university to scrabble his way through Europe and Egypt, also lived with his sister Karen one summer, spent another sharing a house with other students, and moved home again when we were getting ready to leave. He was a big help in painting the bus. Our little pickup truck was easy for him to do after painting the bus.

When he found his own place, it was a small basement suite where a jar of Chicken Delight to dress up a piece of chicken was a common dinner for him. Karen was busy with Marc and her career, Al was working too, so we knew the family was okay.

Keith Herle, B.A., B Sc., CPHI (C), with nine years of post secondary study.

Sunny and humid with a thunderstorm watch for later today. Heading for Richelieu via Montréal. Info centre recommends Highway 40 instead of Highway 20 and we headed right into and through Montréal, directly to our parking spot at the Gravel's home, where we had parked on our previous trip to Montréal. After greetings, we packed an overnight bag and went into Montréal to meet with Serge. Our purpose here this time is to sell this house on Karen's behalf, but first to prepare it for sale before the house is listed and shown.

Another family loss was John's brother-in-law from Camrose, who died after a long illness. Again, it wasn't possible to go home for the funeral.

June 10. We've done floors, walls, Venetian blinds, staining, varnishing. Serge has had the carpets cleaned, and some exterior painting done; the work has gone well. We have taken some time out to visit the Gravels, enjoying Nicole's mother who lives with them for now. We attended their granddaughters' birthday party, and got to say hello to their son Alain when he called from a trip to France. We met Alain earlier when he was an exchange student with our Allan, who in turn had a great stay with the Gravels. Our families really bonded because of that high school program opportunity for our kids.

We learned from talking to Hilary in Vancouver today that our brother Dennis and Maureen's pig roast in Ardrossan, Alberta, has been postponed from July to September. That's great for us, because now we can rearrange our schedule to be there before returning to Vancouver!

Last night the Canucks lost the Stanley Cup to New York, and some rowdies caused a riot in Vancouver!! Bad press for such a beautiful city!

Karen's house is now listed with a real estate agent in Montréal, and we're ready to continue east to see the Atlantic provinces until we have to be back for Karen and Marc.

We finally decided we must purchase a video camera for this very special trip. We certainly were very fortunate to have had the translation help of Nicole to help us make our choice.

June 16. First try with the video camera before we left the campground, and we headed toward the Bathurst, New Brunswick area. Drove through heavy woods, big hills for a couple hours, then gorgeous flat farmlands. Saw beautiful views from hilltops. Saw Sugarloaf Mountain in Campbellton, drove past Bathurst to Chapman's Trailer Park. Ended up parking in the park owner's yard because it was too soft in the campground field beside the sea. Chatty and friendly people. They're so pleasant. The owner told us about a place where we could get a nice lobster dinner, but it was $19.95. Expensive for us, but we made reservations and went anyway. We—especially me!—wanted to get started on the lobster!

We were greeted ever so warmly at Carey's By the Sea, and were introduced to Elizabeth in the kitchen, because she'd come from BC recently. It was like visiting with family to be with her and the owners, Toni and Johnny Carey. Elizabeth took us outside to see the uniquely decorated cabins being fixed up for rentals for this summer. Eccentric, eclectic, and even a rather psychedelic unit were rentals, as well as a very beautifully decorated house. We invited Elizabeth over tomorrow. Toni suggested we drive to the beach up the road and see the sunset from their new property— which we did. Met an older couple there, then a younger couple drove down onto the beach where we were walking, and a girl called out "Who's from BC?" and we all chatted. We're invited to see their place on Paradise Road nearby. Everyone is so friendly!! Watched CTV news—didn't start 'til midnight!!

Friday morning, we slept 'til after 9:00 a.m.! Up and out for a drive back along the coast through small villages east of Bathurst. To the info centre, very friendly service. Saw Tetagouche Falls, the mining museum, Atlas Park, and headed for home. Bought smaller lobsters for supper, picked up Elizabeth and went for a drive to Pokeshaw where the big black cormorants settled on a huge rock bluff, drying their feathers. Returned to the bus with Elizabeth. Alice and Ellsworth, our campground hosts, came in for tea, and said people sure do slow down to look at our *Dragonfly* when they see it parked here by their barn.

Decided on a drive to the Acadian Peninsula the next day. Discovered the Pope's Museum—a replica of the Vatican and St. Peter's Square. Lots of relics, religious habits and portraits of all 260-plus popes. Now we have a little better idea of what our kids, parents, and friends saw when they went to Rome. We've never been anywhere we couldn't drive, but our three kids and my parents have all been to Europe.

The afternoon was spent at the Acadian Village. It is the restoration of homes, boat house, school, church, tavern, store, smithy, print shop, carpentry workshop, and we saw staff in period costumes, doing their appropriate crafts and tasks. We saw shingles being made, nails, linen and woollen items on a loom, and bread baked. There was even an operating flour mill powered by a waterwheel, where the wheat was ground, supplying the flour for the bread that was baked for the employees to eat. All the staff were very bilingual, friendly, and interesting.

We found a 7:00 p.m. Mass to attend, and because it was all in French, and I guess I was really tired or daydreaming, I didn't even recognize the exchange of peace until John nudged me! Home for hamburgers and sleep.

On Sunday we decided to see more of the Acadian peninsula. Such tidy homes, almost all look freshly painted or are being painted. Acadian and Canadian flags everywhere. No fleur-de-lis here! Lots of mosquitoes and blackflies every day. I have lumps on my scalp and John has sores on his legs and arms from these blackflies and skeeters. The critters love John like I love lobster! Drove many miles of coast, beaches, bays, and took a free ferry to Miscou Island in the northeast corner of New Brunswick. We had about a thirty-second wait, drove on, and as we pulled away, I stepped out of the car to be in the fresh air and noticed we were backing up! Sure enough, there on the dock was another car waiting to cross, and the lady captain smiled and nodded hello, and as smooth as can be, she re-docked, loaded one more, and we were away in seconds. Such service!

We toured the little island, saw the oldest lighthouse in operation in the Maritimes, and walked an interpretive boardwalk on a peat bog, peat being quite an industry there. Bought a big lobster for me and a few to clean and freeze so our kids can have a taste. Was it ever a lot of work to clean just those few!! Back at the campground, we discovered we had NO power! Coach batteries dead as a doorknob—John tried boosting each one but isn't hopeful.

June 20. Al's birthday! Another FMCA camper led us into Bathurst to three different places to look for batteries. No luck. Will try in Moncton. Drove only a couple hours to St. Louis de Kent, a nice spot on the eastern coast of New Brunswick, near Kouchibouguac National Park, and settled in a campground that didn't have anyone else in it but the young caretaker and zillions of mosquitoes. We drove beyond the national park to Escuminac to see a seaside monument to thirty-five fishermen lost at sea during a sudden storm in 1959. It was really sad and at the base of the monument was a simple floral arrangement that spelled "Dad" in blue flowers. I remembered that yesterday was Father's Day.

Stopped to call Al for his birthday. It was almost 10:00 pm. for us; 6:00 p.m. in Vancouver. Al wasn't home from work yet, but we had a nice chat with Jenny. Used a private phone in the home/office of the local laundromat. There are no pay phones here. Even the service stations have only private phones, and any business in town will let you use their phone.

We have heard and read about *Le Pays de la Sagouine*—an Acadian novel about the hardships during the '20s and '30s as seen by the heroine, a scrubwoman, and her community. Apparently, it's a novel as well known and loved by the French as *Anne of Green Gables* is to the English. This town of Bouctouche is where the author was born and the setting of the mythical community of the book. The settlement is an island accessible by a long boardwalk over the bay leading to the buildings in the setting of this book. The musicians were playing fiddles, accordions, spoons, and the book's characters were in costume. They were going to present stories in French on the stage. We asked if we could meet the characters and have them tell us a bit about their characters in English. They most willingly and graciously did, otherwise we'd have lost the whole story and wouldn't have gotten much from that tour.

Spent the rest of the day at Kouchibouguac National Park at the sand dunes, salt marshes, forests, lagoons. There were floating sidewalks over sand dunes to the open ocean view! There was almost no one else there—except for the trillions of mosquitoes. The tourist season has not yet started.

Another easy travel day of only one and a half hours to our campground in Shediac, and then we went right to Moncton to buy batteries. The info centre helped us find a place and told us when to come back to see the tidal bore. Next, we went to Magnetic Hill, where John filmed me in the car as it "rolled uphill." Quite the phenomenon, which turns out to be an optical illusion because of the surrounding hills. We returned to Shediac, home of the world's largest lobster (statue) and the info centre there. Bought frozen canned lobster and went for a walk along the beach. We read that the waters here are the warmest north of the Carolinas and we walked a long ways on the wide, beautifully clean, almost-deserted beach. Lots of room to play. Back at the bus, John watched a ball-game on TV in silence so I could concentrate on postcards. I did all twenty-one—for our three kids and 18 brothers and sisters.

Returned to Moncton to see the rush of the tide sweep the river in the opposite direction in the Petitcodiac River. Instead of the usual six-hour tidal change, this tide surges in over a one-hour period only, then goes out for eleven hours. There is parking, bleachers, a promenade on the riverbanks, and an electronic sign at the street to inform us of the next tidal bore. Even had a young fellow from the tourist info centre handing out welcoming brochures with lots of area information included.

After picking up the ordered batteries we went home and John installed them just before a sudden squall blew in. Heavy wind and rain for just a few minutes, but enough to flip our neighbours' awning right over their rooftop with the pole coming through a window on the back side of their trailer, frightening the people inside. Soon the sun shone again and John helped the caretaker get the awning off the roof and remove the hardware. We listened to PEI radio, went out for a seafood supper, picked up developed photos and worked on our photo album.

Insomnia got me up at 4:30 am., so I worked on the album, washed the floor, and swept the rugs. It is a sunny and hot day. Drove to the PEI ferry—excited to go, excited on arrival!! Headed for a campground listed near Charlottetown, which seems to be centrally located. PEI is such a lush bright green and so beautiful with small rocky hills. The trees are really a special shade of bright green and yes, the soil is RED and also turns the water lapping on shore red. Even though I'd heard about them, the fields of green potato plants with their white flowers on the red soil were so much more colourful than I expected.

PEI. Red soil makes the water look red

LUPINES EVERYWHERE along the roadsides. There's every shade of white, pink, purple, and blue. Haven't been this excited about a place for a long time! Went to a community rec hall in New Glasgow for a lobster supper. Six tour buses were there also.

Seats 400. We could choose seafood chowder or steamed mussels for the APPETIZER.

John had the chowder, which came in a big bowl. I got mussels and received a heaping dinner plate of the meatiest mussels I've ever seen! Our waitress came back and asked if we'd like another appetizer and, because it was so good, we said yes, but just half the serving of mussels. I got another huge plateful! The mussels I've had in BC have a speck of meat inside, but these were so full, so fresh because of the mussel beds grown right there. We could have left the table feeling very satisfied at that point, but there were still the salads and the one-pound lobster to come, then pie and cake were served. No wonder the crowds keep coming. Our waitress said she's worked here for eight years and loves her job. After the meal, we did a lot of back-road scenic driving. A memorable introduction to PEI!

Absolutely wonderful!!

Saturday was sunny and beautiful all day. Lazed in the campground, cleaned the car, cut John's hair, chatted with our neighbours, two young families. I just feel so good to be here. Like a goal accomplished and it's so peaceful.

The capital city of Charlottetown has 16,000 people, the city of Summerside has 9,000, and the whole island has only 130,000 population. Being in Summerside reminded me of a silver charm bracelet with letters spelling "Summerside" that was given to me in my teens as a gift by a boy I liked who went there as a cadet.

The roads here have some rough spots, but for this small a place, they're really good. The few people we met certainly were friendly and helpful, but we've spent most of our time in the car, travelling the coastline, having chowder meals at lighthouse restaurants. And taking in the superb views where the waters of the Gulf of St. Lawrence meet the Northumberland Straits on PEI's west coast.

For the next few days, my diary keeping was missed, but the memories are on our video—of the miles of unused beaches, the wonderful surf sounds, the reddest of sunsets, the touring we did of the Anne of Green Gables house, and Lucy Maude Montgomery's home site, hearing the rustling of the leaves so vividly described in the Anne books.

We drove and walked along Cavendish beach—we were surprised that there were sand dunes making about forty miles of continuous beach along the northern curved coastline of PEI. About seven miles of beach was closed just then for the rare piping plover birds who had nested in the area, but there was no shortage of beach, with more than thirty miles still to choose from right there. There is a bit of road for a few miles where the sand drifts over the road like snow on the prairies in the winter.

It was nearly midnight when we returned to our home, and if we weren't so darned tired I would have loved to join a campfire nearby where I could hear them singing a cute song with a chorus that had "She's a big lass, and a bonnie lass, and she likes her beer, and they call her [couldn't hear], and I wish she was here." There was a lot of laughter with the song.

By chance, on Sunday evening, after much more sightseeing, we heard that same song on the car radio. We both loved it. So, on Monday, in a record and tape store, I asked in vain to find that tape with the few words we could remember, until I said we heard it last night on the radio station. When I could tell them which radio station it was, I was told that the radio station was just upstairs and the lady at the desk would be able to help us! Well, we found out that it was Anna McGoldrick singing, but still couldn't identify the song. Looking through tapes downstairs again, the name "Cushie Butterfield" did the trick and has provided many laughs for us as we travel. We now have a few Maritime music tapes and really enjoy them.

Again, like on the Acadian peninsula, all the buildings are so clean—just freshly painted—even the picnic tables in our campground are a fresh bright blue, the washroom doors are pastels. Sure adds to the natural beauty already here. I think I felt sadder than John to leave PEI, I wish we could have stayed longer.

We were being welcomed by bagpipes even as we entered in the wrong direction (because of poor markings in a construction area) at the tourist info centre in Nova Scotia. I'm telling you, it seems like the Maritimes really rolls out the red carpet for its visitors. Our first stop was Pictou, where the lobster is legendary. For the next couple days we learned about the Scottish heritage of the area and toured the town and the Grohmann knife factory.

On the road again, over the Canso Causeway that links Cape Breton Island with the rest of Nova Scotia, and we found our only CCC in Atlantic Canada at Baddeck. After settling, we set off for Rita MacNeil's tea house at Big Pond. I've been wanting to come here too, for years, ever since we saw her perform at Expo 86 in Vancouver with the Men of the Deep. The tea house was closed and undergoing extensive renovations, but we happened to meet and talk to a young girl who had worked there and was certainly a fan of Rita's. She told us Rita visits the tea house very frequently in the summer and chats with her guests. To get to Big Pond, we crossed the huge lake, Bras d' Or, at one place on a ferry that cost 25 cents each way!

July 1. CANADA DAY! Decided to miss all the festivities in town and go around Cape Breton Island on the famous Cabot Trail. It was an all-day excursion, driving the northern coastline of Nova Scotia. Superb scenery and surprises too. On the map we saw Scarecrow Theatre. Not knowing what it was, we didn't get excited about it or think we would attend any theatre until we began seeing unusual scarecrows in driveways and then, suddenly, in a field, beside the road, so many scarecrows—standing, seated, some with masks of famous people and politicians, wearing suits, dresses, old Fortrels, bridal wear, formals, uniforms, work clothes … just everything! Seemed like dozens of them! And the way they were seated, they seemed to be the spectators, the audience, looking at us! What a novel idea!

Scarecrow theatre.

They looked like they were the audience.

John at the Scarecrow Theatre.

So much more spectacular scenery, mountains, whale-watching areas, and excellent signs at the many stops we made that explained the environment and history of each area. Also, we saw an old stone shepherd's hut, reminiscent of the local Scottish heritage. There were some very steep climbs and we were certainly glad we were in the car, not in the bus. Toured a bog area and learned more about moss and its uses. Out of the national park area, we saw more and more lobster cages, as we had seen for the past few weeks. Instead of old cars in the yards, we'd see boats and lobster cages. As we felt bound to our road system, we begin to understand how vital the sea is to the people who lived here.

Saturday. A swim, laundry, Mass, and a visit to the Alexander Graham Bell National Museum. Very impressive—both the inventiveness of Mr. Bell and the very modern building this museum is housed in. He lived in Baddeck for many years, and did a lot more than invent the telephone, especially in communication for the deaf, as his wife was deaf.

Final preparations at home to leave the bus on this site while we go to Newfoundland and stay at bed-and-breakfasts. We can travel much faster by car, and not have to return to the bus each evening. We will take the shorter ferry route to Newfoundland, and drive across the province on the Trans-Canada Highway to St. John's, then meander back. It's the most efficient way we can plan.

Early Sunday morning, we rise and are off to North Sydney for a 9:00 a.m. ferry, a six-hour ride with movies, live entertainment, and passenger mingling. On board, we met a couple who had spent a month in Newfoundland last summer. She said she cried when it was time to leave, so they are going back for the whole summer this year.

When we landed, it did feel like we were on "the rock," as Newfoundland is called, covered with mossy plants and VERY short trees. There are lots of mountains, and even if it was quite foggy for a while, we saw the most unique fishing villages, just as we were told we would. As we took the dead-end road to the east, we saw homes like wooden boxes—painted lime, yellow, pink, aqua, green, blue,—so picturesque. Back toward the ferry and up along Highway 1, we found a place to stay where we had our own cabin, at Carteyville.

We had breakfast in the house with another guest, on his way to fish in Labrador, then we were off along the main highway. We saw really odd shaped mountains as we passed Corner Brook, many lakes and rivers, and it looked like any wide spot in the road was a mighty comfy place to set up camp. Next, we came to Gander.

We've heard so much about the Gander Airport and now we see the poignant memorial of a man holding the hand of a child on each side of him, looking in the direction of where a plane, carrying more than two hundred US soldiers home from Germany, crashed right after take-off on December 12, 1985. One of the visitors there told us she was a cousin of one of the soldiers lost, and said how sad it was to lose so many—and it had nothing to do with a war.

Saw lots more before finding our B&B in St. John's. Did we ever luck out!! It was a beautiful room with a TV (no time to turn it on), and a telephone that we made good use of with our calling card. It was such a treat to have a comfy place from which to make our long-distance calls, and we caught up on a lot of news from home, including the sad news that a close friend, Bill St. Godard, was in palliative care now. We hoped we'd make it home in time to see him again.

The historic harbour of Quidi Vidi is so recognizable, and so lovely to see for real. We continued up to Signal Hill where Marconi sent his first transatlantic wireless message. Just a little later we were in Trepassey, where Amelia Earhart's transatlantic flight originated. What a lot of history here!

Puffins and kitty hawks by the thousands live on the rocks off the eastern coast and bird-watching cruises are big business here. We didn't have the time or the money to spend on a boat cruise to the bird islands, but certainly would like to if we had another chance. Some place names we travelled through are really curious, like Witless Bay. Another town, Ferryland has an archaeological dig going on, as there was at Signal Hill.

There were supposed to be thousands of caribou as we drove the perimeter of the Avalon Wilderness Area on tundra that looked like what we see in pictures of barren Arctic lands—no trees, just flat land, grasses, and ponds. There was a fourteen-mile-long dead-end road we decided to skip to save time and learned later that's where the caribou were! We were also hurrying to see some whales sighted just an hour or two ahead. We arrived in time to see lots of whales spouting and splashing, and people scooping up small fish called capelin that were attracting and feeding the whales. Stopped at a service station snack bar and were given fresh homemade bread with molasses after our meal—as an extra. I was surprised how the molasses tasted like corn syrup! Very light, clear, and sweet. Returned to our B&B, let ourselves in with our house key, relaxed in the living room, and soon our hostess came home too. So trusting!

Wednesday, July 6. Two days left to get back to the ferry. Followed our hostess's advice and visited the Fluvarium in Pippy Park. It is an underwater living gallery and exhibits. Drove to Cape Spears, THE MOST EASTERLY POINT IN ALL OF NORTH AMERICA. And we were really there! As we drove on, we commented that we'd sure hate to be a rock picker in these parts. There are ponds everywhere and they all have names—so much fresh water. Drove through Terra Nova National Park where we heard there might be an iceberg offshore but I guess it was so small, it melted long before we got there. I never realized until folks told us that when an iceberg is near, the temperature is much colder because of the big floating piece of ice. There's almost no farming in Newfoundland as we know it.

Found a B&B in a pub being renovated. It was supposed to be closed, but the fellow opened a room for us for $50. Not cheap. Our beautiful room in St. John's was only $40 and sure beat this place! But we were safe and had a place to sleep.

The second half of the return trip toward the ferry home was made up of many short side trips off Highway 1. We remembered Rose and Tony's anniversary at a stop near Corner Brook, and were wishing we could have a couple or three more days so we could have gone north to Labrador, and see the site of the Vikings' landing north of Gros Morne National Park. Just can't make the time on this trip. If there ever is a next time, I'd also like to go to the French Islands of Saint Pierre and Miquelon.

Our B&B this time was with a wonderful character of a lady who displayed her love for St. Theresa throughout her house. When I mentioned that my mom also especially loved St. Theresa, she said in a big booming voice, "Ah, but it's St. Anthony who rules the roost around here. And he don't come cheap no more, either!" Seems like whenever she asks St. Anthony to help her find a lost item, she's promised to give more money lately in her effort to find these things. When she was watching a hockey game, I asked her if she was a real sports fan. She said no, she was just watching whatever was on TV. You could watch CBC or no TV. Those were the choices. That's the only station there was. She and John played crib while I made some phone calls. When she told John a joke with her strong Newfie accent, John didn't get the punch line. Although he asked her to repeat it once, he was too embarrassed to ask again. Something about a Newfie window washer on a skyscraper and the boss told him to go back up because he missed a window. Anybody know the rest???????

Yes, I felt sad to leave "the rock" of Newfoundland and if there's a time to ever come back, I'd be delighted.

As we drove toward Halifax, we saw Irving gas stations everywhere. They seem to be quite a monopoly. Apparently Irving will set up a service station beside an existing one, offer bargain prices until the competition closes, then raise their prices to whatever they want. At least that's what it seemed like to us from what we see and hear. We settled in Lower Sackville, just north of Halifax, and drove into the foggy city to see Jenny's uncle and aunt. They both have a great sense of humour and we had a very interesting evening. Plans were made for sightseeing the following day.

8:30 a.m. Sunday Mass in Sackville was in a beautiful church that reminded us of the one in Apache Junction in Arizona. Later, Peggy's Cove through a thick fog was still quite impressive, and the fog lessened so we could see Mahon Bay much better. Then to the Ross Farm Museum, where I sat down to milk a cow and actually got some milk into the pail. Not only did I surprise Dorothy, I surprised myself!

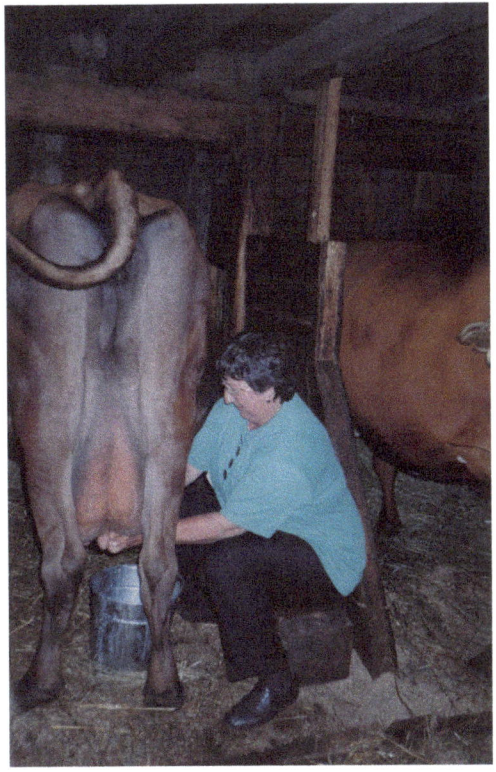

Meanwhile, the boys, John and Michael, were going through the barns, shops, and sheds at their own pace. From there, we were taken to a viewpoint to see the vast tidal flats of the Minas Basin in the Bay of Fundy that is really spectacular in its size. It would be wonderful to see this area in full daylight without fog!

Another sunny day on the road. Lots of porcupine roadkill. In PEI it was skunks—Newfoundland has no skunks at all.

Returned to New Brunswick, settled near Sussex to see Fundy National Park and the famous Hopewell Rocks. Took a chance on trying to reach previous neighbours from Burnaby who moved to Sussex, but their friend said they were back west for the summer, so we're on opposite coasts again.

Near Fundy Park is the town of Alma, and because this area has the highest tides, we were told to see the fishing boats tied up to the dock in the evening, then come back later to see them sitting on dry land when the tide recedes to about a kilometre away from the boats. A very graphic way to see why the boating and fishing is completely dictated by the times of the tides!

While these boats were changing levels, we were visiting the Hopewell Rocks or flowerpot rocks, as they are also called, because the huge rocks are maybe 20 or 30 feet high with trees and vegetation growing on top. That's how we saw them because the tide was out. We didn't see them during high tide because it would be during the night, and we had to leave that day. But, the pictures we saw show these huge rocks submerged by the tide and the trees on top looked like tiny islands. We didn't have any such majestic tide changes on the West Coast where we lived. [In 2016 a storm caused the Hopewell Rocks to collapse, eliminating a very iconic tourist landmark. I am very happy to have seen it well before that.]

Here we also learned it was the Irish who settled these low-lying areas. And we broke off a CB antenna getting around a tight corner when leaving the campground this morning.

Next stop should be Saint John to meet friends from our early Burnaby, BC, days that we haven't seen for about twelve years.

It was an easy drive to a nice campground in the centre of the city in Rockwood Park, and we arranged to meet Ron Smith at 7:00 p.m. and took ourselves to the Reversing Falls—a tidal phenomenon where the river makes a dramatic change of direction every six hours. Had a lovely dinner in the restaurant above the changing river, and later survived locking all three of our keys inside the car when we went for a different view. Thank you, BCAA membership! I had put my purse—with my set of keys and the spare—in the trunk, as well as John's jacket with his keys in the pocket, while we carried the camera, watched, and videotaped the birds feasting as the tide changed so dramatically.

We spent a lovely evening visit and drive with Ron, then picked up Lovina from her work at 10:00 pm. to continue our visit. Here we learned that the Minas Basin we saw with Dorothy and Michael has 52-foot tides and, here at the Reversing Falls, the tide is 28 feet and pushes the river back so forcefully it causes whirlpools and rapids that there is a very limited time each day for boats to pass through! Another interesting thing we saw in the afternoon were the cormorants—the big black birds that would swoop down and eat the food brought in by the tide. They'd ride the fast water a ways upstream, then fly back, land, and let the water carry them upstream again. They had a real floating smorgasbord. Many seals were bobbing in the water too, enjoying their banquet.

All this time we'd been in touch with Karen in Vancouver and our real estate agent Peggy in Montréal, and we had accepted an offer on the house. That was a good feeling!

July 13. Karen's birthday. Ron used his Duraclean method to clean our carpet and upholstery, then we were gone sightseeing with him. We saw the shipbuilding area, some of the Irving empire, and saw the grace and beauty of so many of the old buildings and learned about the Loyalists. In fact, today was the Loyalist Days Parade.

It was a very festive atmosphere and a very nice way to see the townspeople. This parade is unique to the Saint John area. We walked through a park in the centre of town with Loyalist graves from the 1800s, beautiful flower beds among statues, and monuments. A lot of history again. Ron pointed out Partridge Island, where many Irish immigrants are buried because of smallpox and cholera—it was a huge quarantine area. Later, we sat at an outdoor pub table listening to KAMIKAZE KARAOKE until we picked up Lovina from her telephone office job at 10:00 p.m. and visited with her again for a while.

Changing time zones once again as we leave New Brunswick and cross the border into the United States. (We have at least six digital clocks on board on various appliances and I'm learning to change some of them without their instruction manuals.) Lots of rocks and tundra, and then beautiful gardening areas. We see lovely potato and other vegetable fields. Brown-eyed Susies are alongside the road. Through the towns of Bangor and Mexico, as we travel in Maine on "The Airline" route, as I think it's called. We're listening to our Maritime tapes and grinning as we drive. We chose a campground in the White Mountains area in New Hampshire and spent the most we'd ever spent so far for a night: $21 in US dollars that turned out to be $29 in Canadian—according to them!

Through pretty New England towns and into Vermont, we returned to Canada and chose a budget campground south of Montréal. But the power was so poor that we stayed one night only and went a half mile further to a KOA we had checked out before. It was rather expensive, but had all the amenities we really wanted because tomorrow we would have Karen and Marc with us for ten days!!

July 16. Found our way to Dorval airport, and saw Karen and Marc's smiles beaming at us as they came off their flight. Almost the first words Marc said were, "Now, let's go to OUR bus!" He was three years old in April and sure didn't forget about us in the past two months.

The next few days are a happy blur, best recalled by us on video. The real estate wound up very slowly, final touch-ups to the house were done, meetings and appointments kept. Karen was able to use our car a lot and we got to keep Marc a lot. It was very hot and humid and we were either in the pool or in the AC bus during the hottest part of the day. Marc loved eating "poksicles" and watching Disney videos. We also had Serge and his family members and our friends, the Gravels, over for a visit at our place, and then Serge, John, Marc, and I spent a day at Parc Safari. And the house sale was completed.

SOLD. John worked to get Karen's Montréal house ready for sale.

Too soon it was July 27 and we took Karen and Marc back to the airport, and moved to the Gravels' yard again to prepare for a "mini-vacation" north of Québec City with Jacques and Nicole.

On board were Jacques and Nicole, and Nicole's mother as we headed north past Québec City to Charlesbourg where Nicole's mother would be staying with her son and daughter-in-law for the next few months. After a very brief stop there, we continued north, past the famous shrine of Sainte-Anne-de-Beaupré and the Mont-Sainte-Anne ski area where we had stayed with the Gravels a few years ago, all the way to Baie-Saint-Paul. John and Jacques got the bus parked in such a tight spot it looked like they airlifted it in there. This area is really an artist's dream. Rolling hills and steep roads really made our bus live up to its Dragonfly name as we dragged ourselves up the sharp climbs and we flew with ease on the down side.

Oh, this town of Baie-Saint-Paul is so pretty! There are very brightly coloured buildings, like yellow, hot pink, purple, and orange. There are monumental churches, homes from the 1600s, stone buildings, narrow streets, ornate wrought-iron railings, like we saw on Bourbon Street in New Orleans. The Angelus bells were ringing at noon here as I remembered from my younger years in Alberta.

I must tell you now about a much-anticipated return trip. We drove the countryside by car, revisiting a special church at St. Joseph-de-la-Rive! I was so happy to have a chance to see that old church again. I can't explain the connection that I felt there except to say that it gave me a special sense of comfort. I'm not sure that I could ever adequately describe how it made me feel so at peace. I am so grateful to have been able to revisit this particular church.

The building itself is just a small, humble wooden church but very, very old and inside it has a theme relating to the sea. At the entrance, the holy water font is a large seashell. The baptismal font is a HUGE seashell shape. The altar is set on two crossed anchors. Fishes are carved along the edge of the altar, and the communion rail is a heavy rope. The pews and carpets are sea-green, and a large wooden mural on the wall has waves carved into it. The Stations of the Cross are intricately carved of wood, and there's a picture of a sailing ship on the wall. This time we had the video camera to record it, so I will see it again.

Returning to Baie-Saint-Paul, there was time to drive to the wharf for a walk along the beach. After the hot day and all the walking we did, Nicole giggled when she walked on the beach and said, "It feels like sandblasting for the feet." Then the sun set and for the thousandth time since early June, we were attacked by blackflies and/or mosquitoes and, once again, looked like we were doing the Mexican hat dance without the hat or even music! We were trying to swat everywhere at once!

We were in mountains as big as the foothills of the Rockies as we continued north with the bus. We saw people at the roadsides picking low-bush sweet blueberries. Fresh blueberry pies have been noted for sale on signs in this area. Hills are steeper—11 and l2 percent grades sure make John wish our Jake brake was already installed. We followed the beautiful edge of the St. Lawrence River for many miles at times, seeing the arched roof lines of the houses, curved at the eaves. Our next destination was again picture-perfect. Jacques and Nicole directed us to the ferry dock at Saint-Siméon, where we backed into a serviced site with only a road between us and the beautiful expanse of an ocean view. The St. Lawrence River is so wide it looks like the ocean. It would have been nice to just sit there for days, but our time was limited, so after lunch, we went even further north to Baie-Sainte-Catherine and to the Saguenay River. By now, we were seeing beluga whales and the whale-watching cruise ships in the area.

We crossed the Saguenay River by ferry and then drove around Tadoussac, yet another very picturesque town. We walked through the *trés élégante* Hotel Tadoussac and a very old native church, dating back to the 1600s, as well as a trading post museum. There we also saw sand dunes, so big that in the 1920s, people would ski down them on regular skis. But this was discontinued in the 1930s for the protection of the dunes and the safety of the people.

We drove east to Sacré-Coeur and saw another majestic natural view along the Saguenay River. I really got to like poutine—not sure of how to spell it, but I like to eat it! It's French fries with gravy and cheese curds. Had some today. Returned to our idyllic campsite by the Saint-Siméon ferry dock and watched the boat lights on the water. Ah, the sweet life!

July 31. Keith's birthday. We've been phoning him at the three different birthday dinners he's being treated to.

It's an early rise for the line-up procedure for the two-hour sailing across the St. Lawrence to Rivière-du-Loup on the Gaspé Peninsula. A very pleasant crossing; we saw Rabbit Island and more beluga whales. About five hours of driving back to Richelieu and the mini-vacation is over for the four of us.

More pampering and family visiting at the Gravels. Nicole even made bread pudding for John who loudly complains that I hardly EVER make it for him.

Got a new little table installed in our living room. We had ordered it from a craftsman in the area before Karen came to visit. Our final day in Québec.

I had insomnia and waves of sadness as we were heading back home to realize that neither Mom nor Dad would ever be there again. Nicole and I shared a cry before we left. We drove about three hours into New York State in the Adirondack mountains. It's a heavily wooded area with lots of streams, lakes, summer water sports, and ski hills. Both of us are very tired. Exits are not marked by the mile, and we think we got ripped off on our first tank of diesel fuel because we still had only Canadian dollars. We don't usually let ourselves be without the local currency when we cross borders, but it happened and we felt grumpy. Found our CCC, and went for a drive to get US money, Minwax to stain our new table, car gas, and beer. Now we're ready, but too tired to walk. Went to bed to read at 9:00 pm. It's been very hot and humid, and looks steamy outside. We keep thinking it's going to rain.

In the morning, we were very tired and unpleasant to each other, turned up the music so we couldn't talk to each other. Drove further south, then west, still in New York, then south again into Pennsylvania, then west again on I-80. There were so many trucks, so much construction, so much smog, such poor visibility toward what were probably beautiful hills on a clear day. Many forests, valleys, small farms. The cities along the way seem to have a lot of manufacturing plants. Decided to take a chance at a truck stop at Snowshoe in a sparsely populated area about 4:30 p.m. Filled the gas tank for the generator, turned on the AC, and started feeling a lot better. We watched the trucker beside us set out his own little tabletop barbecue on the ground and grill his own hot dogs! We chatted with him about his truck, which was a very fancy new rig, and even had a little fridge in the sleeping compartment that he showed us.

We used our fresh basil and other toppings on a pizza, and with the bread pudding and maple syrup from Jacques and Nicole, we had a very nice supper in our free rest area. Finally the heavy rains came, but with the generator and the AC running all night, we hardly heard it.

Heavy rains continued the next day as we drove through forest reserves and small farms. The windshield is leaking like it did once before. Drove only 179 miles to our next CCC.

Just before our turnoff, we saw an Amish horse and buggy crossing over us on an overpass. We were delighted, because we hoped to see the Amish here. The afternoon was spent driving by car, marvelling at their farms. The Amish farmhouses are plain white, though many have colourful flower beds. There are no curtains, all have dark-green blinds. They have no electricity or phone or cars on their farms. There are beautiful horses and buggies, and John was very interested in seeing the horse-drawn farming equipment like the manure-spreaders, binders, ploughs, cultivators. We saw them all! The grain fields were all stooked so neatly. We stopped at a couple of the roadside stands and chatted with the Amish farmers and bought their produce—peaches, vegetables, fresh bread, apple pie that was SO good, and cinnamon buns. Had a great Amish supper. Managed to put two coats of stain on our little table today.

Stayed home the next day and got caught up on all the mail, odd jobs, and the day seemed to fly by until suddenly it seemed it was time to go for 5:00 p.m. Mass in Mercer. A relaxing evening; phoned Steve and Carol where some family had gathered before those going fishing to Quadra Island were gone. Spoke with a few of my siblings Carol, Rose, Hil, and Ken.

Our neighbour here is an old fellow who speaks very slowly and we got to talking about the weights of our RVs. He said he weighed seventeen tons and we're sixteen tons! Because he's a fifth wheel, he shouldn't weigh near that much. I asked him how come he was so heavy—did he carry rocks? And he said "Y-e-a-h, Ah got so-ome rocks. Ah'll show y-a a ve-ry rare ro-ock." And he proceeded to bring out a red-and-black leopard rock that he said came from Old Mexico. Again, I think I want to do some lapidary work someday.

On the road early in the sunshine, heading across Ohio on the turnpike, on a very lovely direct route straight west. It seems like a well forested area with a lot of corn crops. Easily passed Cleveland, blew a kiss to Max Klinger from *M*A*S*H* as we passed Toledo. Toll was $10.80 for the Ohio Turnpike, and really worth it. Interesting seeing so many different license plates. Crossed into Indiana on a toll road in great condition. Lower diesel price here: $1.049. No sites left at the Plymouth CCC, but for $10 a night, they gave us one of their Good Neighbour sites. John and I are both very tired, no fraternizing with neighbours tonight. Two more coats of varnish on the new table by now. Lots of seed corn and vegetables grown here.

We took a back road into Nappannee, saw no buggies on the road. Found and toured a motorhome factory, the Newmar Corporation. Again, too rich for us, but are they ever beautiful. Apparently the cabinetmakers are the skilled Amish. Found a Dutch flea market with rows of buggies for sale. Got close-ups with the video. Bought cream pie and bread. Went to Amish Acres, a typical Amish farm. Bought a passport ticket for a tour, dinner, buggy ride, and the theatre. But there was really heavy thunder, lightning, and rain, so we just had the Thresher's Dinner. Excellent. For dessert, I had shoofly pie, John had peanut butter pie. Will return tomorrow in better weather to finish the tour. Back at the bus, we were sure relieved to see that our new Fan-Tastic Vent worked and closed automatically when the rain started, even if we weren't there. Accepted neighbours' invitation to join their campfire; felt good to need long pants and to feel chilly. Seems like it's been so hot and humid for weeks.

We said goodbye to our campfire friends as they left. This was their first time in an RV. They had only tented before and loved having a fridge and a toilet. Their friends rented this to them and they were all waving real friendly as they drove away—and drove right over their own garbage bag!

We returned to Nappannee and had our Amish home tour and the buggy ride that was cancelled by yesterday's storm. Got our tickets for the show *Plain & Fancy,* a Broadway musical that has been playing there for eight months a year for the past eight years. We had enough time to drive around the Amish country-side before the theatre show and found a restaurant called Come and Dine, which we did. We thoroughly enjoyed the play about a young, fun-loving New York couple who came to see the farm they inherited, how the Amish accepted them, and how their contrasting habits were introduced and handled. It's a very funny yet tender comedy. Another wonderful day.

On the road early again. On Highway 30, we passed through a scuzzy section of south Chicago, and felt much better when we were on Highway 80 going west again. Huge crops in such perfect rows. Crossed the mighty Mississippi into Iowa. Third state today. Indiana, Illinois, now Iowa. Saw waterways sculpted into cornfields to prevent erosion. Got to Art and Millie's by 5:00 p.m., earlier than we had planned. Art and Millie are friends from our winter in Texas; she was my partner for the school tutoring we did there.

John and Art got up early the next morning to go to Hawkeye for coffee with the local boys for 6:30 am.!! After a more respectable hour and breakfast, we toured this northeast corner of Iowa and were shown some most amazing things today.

In Spillville are the Bily Brothers clocks. The two brothers were corn farmers by summer and master wooden clock carvers by winter. They donated the entire collection of their hand-carved clocks to the town and asked that the collection never be broken up or sold. Their lifetime of painstaking carvings of clocks are totally made of wood, so amazing—a priceless collection. They are kept in a humidity-controlled house with its own history, too. Antonin Dvorak, the composer, spent the summer of 1893 in this Czech community that his friends in New York recommended so highly.

Saw Ray Bolger's alma mater in Fayette. Saw a special tombstone in a Lima cemetery—a life-size carving of a devoted hired man with his gun and dog. We were told that it was commissioned by the farmer's daughter and certainly is an outstanding tribute. Saw the artificial lake that eliminated two towns, and the Ironclad store to see the first gasoline tractor that went backwards and forwards. Heard a multitude of fascinating stories, both legend and true. Returned home tired and happy.

We'll take Art's suggestion and go west on Highway 3 to West Bend and see the grotto there. On the way, corn fields were still everywhere, we passed through Readlyn. The sign said the population was 857 friendly people and one old grump. A free campsite was available and comfy at the Grotto. What a sight there!! We certainly did not expect such a huge place! It was founded in 1912 and being worked on to this day. Its geological value is millions because it is made up of small rocks, gems. geodes, and agates from all over the world. I still love the amethysts. The statues are of Italian Carrara marble. Beautiful music played as we climbed among the chapels, and very informative free tours were given frequently. This should be a must-see in Iowa. You sure don't have to be religious to appreciate the beauty and peace of this place.

We are seeing flooded fields and high creeks as we continue. Corn is as "high as an elephant's eye" or a tanker truck. Crossed into Minnesota, went into Adrian to see more "Texas" friends, Clarence and Audrey. We went to 5:30 p.m. Mass with them, then to a restaurant and met some of their friends. Served the last of the Québec ice cream with the maple-sugar chunks in it for dessert in our home. Said goodbye so we could leave early in the morning.

Clarence and Audrey were up early to wave, even if it was only 7:15 a.m. as we left town. A few blocks later, there was Clarence in his truck, coming toward us to wave one more time. He's full of surprises. Sunny, but very cool today. The landscape changed dramatically from flat to hilly and rocky with more cattle. Still lots of corn. As we entered South Dakota, the first rest area had a great info centre. There we found a new concept in tour guiding on cassettes!

We rented a package of six cassettes for $20 that would describe South Dakota as we travelled, then we could return them for a $15 refund as we left South Dakota. This was a very good investment. We felt as if we had a tour guide riding with us for the whole week in South Dakota, with a very pleasant voice and lots of extra information across the entire state.

The Corn Palace was the next stop. It was an exhibition building that now gets a fresh exterior coating of corn every year. Intricate patterns of cobs, kernels, seeds, and grasses covered the exterior and formed murals inside as well. Very interesting. We were seeing signs for Wall Drug when it was still 181 miles away. Wall Drug is a huge drugstore/novelty store built on a reputation of offering free ice water to thirsty, hot travellers more than 50 years ago, and just keeps on growing. There's still free ice water, too.

After we crossed the Missouri River we marvelled at the ranch lands. The vast lands of *Dances With Wolves* are all around us now as we arrive at Hart Ranch, the number One Coast to Coast Campground this year. We want to stay a week and see why this CCC is so highly rated. We now know even a week is not enough time for this area as there's SO much to see and do here. A whole summer here would be so nice.

It was a heat wave in mid-August as we toured Badlands National Park. Such vast spectacular scenery; some places looked like lunar moonscapes. There were huge pillars of jagged rock, and coloured layers in the hills representing different eras. For more than 30 miles long, and maybe 20 miles wide, at every bend in the road would be another awesome sight. Just when we thought we must have seen it all, and we couldn't be surprised any more, we were—time and time again!! We watched the storm clouds build during the day and when we got home, we discovered a lot of rain had come through the windows we'd left open in the bus. The heat wave made quick work of drying the cushions again.

We spent the next day being busy at home! Stayed inside with the AC on. We weathered a tornado warning, and decided we'd better go to the bathrooms designated as tornado shelters when the TV advised us to take shelter NOW. Steady thunder, terrific lightning, winds, rain, and when we returned to the bus, the TV kept us informed of the tornado path and we were all safe.

We are excited to go to the Black Hills area now. Our first look at Mount Rushmore was a real rush! Who hasn't wanted to see that? The visitor's centre there is excellent and the carved mountain is just like the pictures we've seen. Its history and construction are awesome. From there we went to see Crazy Horse, a carving being done on a much larger scale. When I say carving, it's really blasting—but over the years, the blasting has gotten accurate to within a fraction of an inch. An entire mountain will become the shape of a native Indian on horseback. This project is ahead of schedule because of the favourable weather, and the museum and display of native dancing were very colourful and enjoyable. A big bin of rocks that had been blasted was available at the exit, so I have my own piece of Crazy Horse.

From there, we travelled a twisty "pigtail" route with roads that cross over each other, and tunnels so narrow that the tour buses are said to have a quarter-inch clearance for their mirrors when

117

they go through. We followed a bus and saw that he had to back up a couple times to make a hairpin turn. We were happy we were just in our car for the sightseeing. Then through Custer State Park, where "the deer and the antelope" and the bison roam. Lots of them. Lots more *Dances With Wolves* kind of countryside. There were so many other highlights about this area.

On another drive, we visited a very well-preserved sod house, built into the east side of a hill to protect the home from the storms that come from the west and north. It was well furnished according to its time, and fascinating to see that it was so well cared for. A root cellar, an outhouse and a machine shed were also complete. We saw a lot of wild turkeys and prairie dog towns in that area too. I wonder how different the prairie dogs are from the gophers at home. I'd never seen a wild turkey before, but grew up raising tame turkeys for our special meals.

I finally chose a day to go to the pool for water exercises at 8:00 am. Turned out to be the only time I spent in the pool in that whole week! Why are we so busy? Another storm is predicted for noon again. Still in a heat wave.

Our little jug of ice water is between us again, to drink as it melts, on a little side trip to Devil's Tower in Wyoming, a natural phenomenon of a huge rock standing alone that looks like a mountain made up of a bundle of rock needles, all upright. We stood awhile in awe, to watch the adventurous progress of the rock climbers.

We had no idea that so much gambling went on outside Reno or Las Vegas in the west. But Deadwood, in South Dakota's Black Hills area, is an old mining town resurrected by gambling and really growing fast. Our brochures said Kevin Costner liked the area so much when he filmed *Dances With Wolves*, that he bought a dress shop in Deadwood, and turned it into the Midnight Saloon and Jake's, the upstairs restaurant. Very up to date. Almost next door is an historic place dedicated to Wild Bill Hickock. There is a lot to remind us of Tombstone, Arizona. A drive up Mt. Moriah to see the graves of Wild Bill, Calamity Jane, and Potato Creek Johnny is a must if you like western history as much as John does. Another very full day.

This was Saturday, we did some catch-up housework, then off to the reptile house, which I enjoyed more than I thought. It's John who is so interested in reptiles! Had to get a pass to come back to finish this tour, in order to go for the black gold jewellery that I love so much and still make it to 5:00 p.m. Mass in Rapid City. We bought a pendant for me, necklace and earring sets for Jenny and Sandy, earrings and pin for Karen, and a necklace for our godchild, Lindsey. Makes me feel so good because I really wanted these for our girls for Christmas. After Mass, we finished the tour of the reptile house, then home to roast beef au jus, cooked on the delay and automatic settings of the micro-convection oven. It turned out very well. I am certainly glad I used this way of cooking today!

August 21. Phoned Keith and Sandy for their first wedding anniversary before we left South Dakota, heading west and north. We stopped at Sturgis, home of the motorcycle rally, to buy a T-shirt for Al. For the last weeks—and next weeks—we would see motorcycles by the hundreds on the highway, and we sure wondered where they were all heading. Now we, too, know about the Sturgis Rally. Next, we went through Spearfish, home of the Passion Play, which we also have to leave for another trip. Some tense moments as we climbed to 5,000 feet and our engine temperature got dangerously high. Needed the AC a lot. Drove through a bit of Wyoming, heading for Little Bighorn in Montana, where General Custer met his Waterloo. Found a unique campground with a big circle of teepees, and parked with them. Made a lovely photo!! Little Bighorn was a large, hilly area, well marked with hundreds of white crosses to mark the spots where the US Cavalry soldiers fell.

We learned of a pow-wow just a few miles away and tried to attend. It was so crowded with teepees, cars, horses, people, that as we inched our way through the throngs, unable to find even a tiny parking spot for our small car, we eventually followed a line of cars to the nearest exit and went back home to Dragonfly, and slept very well amongst those teepees.

Bus in teepee circle.

Driving north in Montana; rocky, mining, wide open spaces. It's so hot and dry. Soon it got flatter, but our elevation was 4,100 feet and the engine temperature was way up again. Good ranching land began to show, then big fields near Great Falls. The contour farming on the gentle slopes looked like quilt blocks from a distance. We were near enough to the Canadian border to cross before settling down at the first campsite we'd find. That turned out to be in Milk River, and though we were very satisfied with it, Isabelle tells us we really missed an interesting visit to the tourist info centre next door. We didn't even think of going there, because we were not in need of any more info. After being treated to a beautiful sunset, we went to sleep.

Elevation is well over 3,000 feet, and it's cooler. Seeing irrigation, canals, harvest in progress, swathers, combines, bales, and stacks of hay. It's a very windy day.

The past six days were filled by visiting with relatives. Never a dull moment! Again, we were on our familiar spot at the Blatz house, surrounded by fun and relatives.

Visited with John's sister, Ann Kuefler, in Camrose yesterday and today. We parked at the Camrose City Campground again. Cousins Roman and Leon were able to come for a breakfast visit. Soon we left for our other parking spot at my sister Rose and Tony's place in Ardrossan—and I had a throbbing toothache. The next few days I had teeth pulled, but between those appointments we drove to see our friends in Marwayne, Al and Doreen, and bought a supply of Ukrainian sausages in Mundare.

We made it to the pig roast at Dennis and Maureen's new home! It was a whopping success for a very full two days.

Dennis and Maureen building a house.

Celebrating with a pig roast.

From a beautiful sunny day on the first day to a drenching rain and muddy yard on the second day, we all enjoyed the festive air just because we were together, and just because my brother Dennis and Maureen's house was so close to being finished. So many fun things happened, including the human tug-of-war to get my youngest brother Pat and Tammy's van out of the muddy lawn so they could go home on the second day.

After the festivities and the Labour Day weekend were over, we came home to see our families and our terminally ill friend, Bill St. Godard, in Palliative Care. We managed a few visits with Bill before John was a pallbearer at his funeral on September 20.

October flew by with many dental appointments for me, and we took Marc to Beachwood (our home CCC in Blaine, Washington) as much as we could and had many dinner invitations to see our friends here before we would leave again.

An aunt in New Jersey made a trip to New York a very exciting reality and, on November 5, I was part of a family group of seven to see New York City and Aunty Pauline. My brother Hil and Sandra, brother Stan and Irene, my sister Lucy, her friend Jackie, and I went. A big city could not be less interesting to John, who preferred to stay home. We saw and did as much as we could fit in for that week until November 12. We saw the Statue of Liberty, Ellis Island, the World Trade Center, the New York Stock Exchange, the Empire State Building, and two Broadway shows. We rode the subway in downtown Manhattan, NYC transit buses, NJ transit, took Aunty Pauline to restaurants, went to Central Park, Bloomingdale's, Tiffany, Trump Tower, and attended Mass at St. Patrick's Cathedral. If you've never been to New York City, we have a two-hour video, made by Stan, that could convince you to go. New York City is wonderful and alive; there is something for everyone to enjoy.

While I was there, there was a message for John to see the family doctor before we leave for Arizona on November 15.

Our early Christmas dinner at Al and Jenny's house was November 13. Jenny even put up a little tree in the family room, and had Christmas touches throughout, carols playing, and a lovely table set. Karen and Sandy brought their special contributions for the dinner table. We had a lovely evening and said our goodbyes to our kids for the winter. Such was not to be.

Two days later, what was supposed to be John's last visit to the doctor for the year became the first of many to diagnose and treat his prostate cancer. Almost three months later, we don't have a surgery date yet.

Although there is time for a quick holiday between some appointments, John says we'll stay here and finish this session, then spend the summer seeing Alaska. So, that's Plan A for the summer. We always have a Plan B to cope with whatever life hands us. There is never a shortage of things to do, but not always the energy or space to do those things when it's cold or rainy. Again, all those family and friends around here are superb. We have a rather full social calendar, and certainly enjoy the visiting. John has also gotten involved with Ken, making wine, and the results are very taste-worthy. For me, just learning to handle this word processor and doing these letters is using up a lot of my time. John is replacing some shelves with drawers and hopefully will add shelves to some cupboards. As I said, we never lack things to do.

Right now, we have a phone in *Dragonfly* at the KOA campground in Surrey. It's the same campground that we stayed in last winter during Mom and Dad's final months. The phone system isn't the greatest, as it seems to be overloaded a lot, and you need a touch tone phone to call us. We can't make long-distance calls from here, so we still need to use pay phones or call from someone else's home. Our plan for now is to probably be here until the end of March, or until John is ready to go again.

Early this morning John got up to check our awning because it didn't sound good in the wind. We had the screen room attached to all three sides of the awning and that survived the Texas and Yuma winds but not so today in Surrey. It's light enough outside by 5:30 am. that John could see our awning had already torn about five feet along the edge so we had to get out of a nice warm bed to take down the entire screen room and roll up the awning in near-freezing weather (about 2 degrees C) then back into that nice warm bed and try to warm up again! *#%*°*%#

It still may take a week or two to know what's happening to John. He says now that he knows he has cancer, he just wants it out, and that's our focus for now.

Dealing With John's Cancer

It's been awhile since I sent out a newsletter—didn't even send Christmas cards, not a single one! This has been quite a typical Vancouver winter, cool and rainy. Though it's true we made this bus so we could live in sunshine each winter, for the second winter in a row we're here to deal with cancer.

Last year we lost both Dad and Mom in April, and now John has been diagnosed with prostate cancer. We do expect a total removal of his cancer and plan on many more years of travel after we deal with this. We have several friends and relatives who have been great support and role models with their success stories of having dealt with this type of cancer. In each case, their lives were loused up for a while, but they are back to "living their lives" again. So, I guess we just have to wait it out. It's the waiting that is the pits.

From November 15, 1994—right after we'd celebrated our early Christmas so we could get to a warm winter—when John was first told about a nodule that needed investigating, a biopsy was done

November 28. On December 16, the cancer was confirmed. A subsequent bone scan is clear: no metastasis. A CT scan is being done next month, with results to come by the end of January. Then it's off to the cancer clinic for a second opinion before a surgery date is set. So, here we are … That's why I couldn't write before Christmas. We had no idea of what was next!

We had a chance meeting with some friends of Mom's and Dad's while shopping in Safeway one day around Christmas; they were surprised to see us still in the area for the winter. Through conversation, they offered us a place to park on their hay farm, where a mobile home had been removed. There was electricity, water, and a septic tank in place—all we had to do was prepare the site for our bus. We went to see it and loved the farm site.

A load or two of gravel on the parking site and cleaning of the septic tank was all that was needed, and we had a parking spot for whenever we were staying in our home area. We got a permanent phone number again, so we could just plug into the new outlet. Messages could be left anytime now and we could change our answering-machine greeting, giving info of where we might be and for how long. It was a very generous offer.

John was also given the riding mower for $1 to mow the yard when there. We just had to sell the mower back to Frank Burm for the same $1 when we didn't need the spot anymore. It was a handshake agreement, and no money was ever exchanged. We would pay the telephone and power bills and were so grateful for this arrangement.

Cardiology tests showed that John wasn't a good candidate for surgery, so it would be radiation treatments for six weeks, Monday to Friday. For one of his first tests, he was told to do some walking during the time he was wearing a Holter monitor. It was winter, snow was on the ground, the road was icy, and though he was careful, he slipped dangerously while crossing over one of the big wide speed bumps in the RV park, making him angry when he came in. He told me that when he returned the Holter the next day, he asked the technician, "Does it record my voice as well as my heart rate?" When she said no, he said, "That was a good thing because it wasn't nice what I said when I slid on some ice!"

It's been such a full winter that some of our friends who live here don't know that we didn't get away for this season. Because we aren't making any miles this winter again, we should be ready for a long trip by spring, so we are talking about a trip to Alaska for the summer. June to August or so …

It was a nice diversion for John to arrange what was needed to settle into our rural location in the Cloverdale area. In March, John began his radiation treatments which lasted into May '95. From our location, we drove to the cancer clinic near Vancouver General Hospital five days a week. John had to drink a quart of water before each radiation treatment, so we said he would drink and I would drive! We had to find humour in dark places sometimes, but it worked for us. One lasting beautiful memory from those daily drives was seeing the cherry trees along Oak Street in Vancouver begin to blossom, then burst open in full bloom as the days went on.

During that time, we interrupted the routine with a real surprise sixty-fifth birthday party for him in May, when about 125 friends and family came to a little hall in Surrey, where John was toasted and roasted just a little. He had told me he didn't want a sixth-fifth birthday party because he wasn't sure how he would be feeling with his radiation treatments. But he really didn't have a say in the matter, and we sure enjoyed planning the surprise party. Our kids and daughters-in-law made the evening special with a potluck supper and a DJ who provided the dance music. When John was asked to give a little speech after we did our talks and congratulations, he expressed his amazement, "I am so surprised to see this many people here because I honestly didn't realize I had this many friends."

Five weeks instead of the usual six weeks later, John had a good check-up result and we were off to Alaska! Another trip on our list of desired places to go while in the Dragonfly. So, at last I will write …

Notes From on the Road to Alaska

Dear friends and family,

Our trip to Alaska was another long—several months—road trip and once-in-a-lifetime experience ... except that this was at least our third once-in-a-lifetime experience!

By mid-June, John was feeling strong enough, confident enough to start this next trip. We were ready to leave Surrey for Chilliwack to visit some Herle family for a couple of days. By Father's Day morning, we met our friends, Jack and Muriel Gleadle, in their bus, *Flyin' High,* and travelled together toward Williams Lake to stay at the farm of my cousin George, living with his son Perry and Tina. George was excited to welcome us and told us about the deer and the bears in the area; before we left two days later, we had seen several deer, a moose, and a bear. George had not lived on a farm all the years I knew him, but now he seemed to have a renewed purpose in life since he lost his wife. Now he was busy building fences, sheds, caring for the animals. It was a new man we were seeing.

We also saw that the poplar trees had been stripped of leaves by an army of caterpillars that spring, making some of the bushes look like the bare trees in fall instead of the beautiful green of spring. It was sad to see the loss of beauty that could have been, because we had seen so much lush greenery already. While in the area, we went to Horsefly to see the young couple who bought our backhoe, business, and truck. They moved the equipment to their ranch, where both machines are being very useful. The young ranchers sure love their new life in the country, and their faces show it.

We drove to the ghost towns of Quesnel Forks and Likely, a town we'd heard about many years ago from that late friend, Bill St. Godard. It was a dry year, and in a hotel bathroom the reality hit when a sign above the toilet stated they were saving water, so please, "If it's yellow, let it mellow. If it's brown, flush it down."

On our way back to the main highway on a good paved road, we heard a BANG as though we'd been shot! John's first thought was that the car fell off the tow hitch. I thought something hit us hard and we had a lot of damage. John stopped, got out, looked everywhere—no damage seen—until he checked the tires and found an inside dual tire had no air. So, after four years of travel, we now know what a blown tire sounds like, and it's scary. We drove slowly into Quesnel to Kal Tire, where the spare tire was efficiently put on and a replacement ordered from PRINCE GEORGE to be ready for us in WILLIAMS LAKE after we toured BARKERVILLE. Such good service and efficiency! Very little loss of travel time that way. We are very grateful to be continuing north without having to make additional miles.

June 20. Remembered Al's birthday as we toured through the restored old town of Barkerville. The tour guides and townspeople were dressed in period garb and even the general store was equipped with goods as it would have been long ago. The rice and lentils I bought were put into cloth drawstring bags. The town had its colourful characters well portrayed as they told about the days of the gold rush. We needed a full one and a half days to see Barkerville. Our new tire was ready for us in Williams Lake so we could continue going north through Prince George and then west. We happened to choose a campground in Houston, still in BC. Through conversation with the likeable owner, John determined that this man's brothers and sisters walked through the Herle farm to go to school in Denzil, Saskatchewan, before this man's family moved to Onaway, Alberta, where he was born. The two fellows had a really good visit that evening.

The next day we reached Meziadin Lake at the south end of the Stewart-Cassiar Highway. Our camping sites were on the lakeshore. The water was so clear, so still, reflecting so much beauty of the trees and sky. What a picture-perfect spot! We and the Gleadles were parked right up to the edge of that beautiful lake.

It was still early enough in the day that we decided to take the side trip to Stewart, and then the tiny town of Hyder, Alaska. No border crossing, just go. There are very few miles of road into Alaska here, but we drove most of them to see the Salmon Glacier on a very rough mining road, where signs told us that we were continuing at our own risk. We drove as far as we dared and I think neither couple would have gone that far without the other, because it's a very lonesome feeling to be so isolated on a very rough road in glacier country.

The Bear Glacier before Stewart and the Salmon Glacier just past Hyder were the first of many wonderful sights to come.

By now, the trees were getting very short—but there were still plenty of them. We were noticing the longer days. We were still able to read at 11:00 p.m. with no lights on! There were four gravel stretches marked on the map on this highway and I drove the car separately through most of that to prevent the gravel from spitting on the car and pitting it. Jack and Muriel thought differently, kept their car in tow, and later bought new headlights to replace smashed ones because their car was hit with a lot of gravel on those miles.

There was a bit of rain as we saw snow-capped mountains, patchy and bare areas of some replanted forests, huge and beautiful lakes popping into view as we drove on switchbacks and hairpin turns to the Stikine River bridge, and then a wilderness resort advertised as we slowly climbed up again. By now, the car was plastered with mud and grit and there was no hint of its true colour. Jack said on the CB that if we'd gone south instead of north we could be in Guatemala by now. He calls this the "No Pleasure Highway." John calls it the "Highway from Hell." But they still have no idea of what is yet to come!

This has been a good road, just too frequently punctuated with washboard and loose gravel. Terrible for the towed cars. The highway is undergoing extensive road improvements for next year's fiftieth anniversary of the Alaska Highway.

Lo and behold, a car wash at the service station where the Stewart-Cassier meets the Alaska Highway. Five dollars for all the water we needed to clean the entire bus and car. And a line-up for the privilege of doing so!

But happy people everywhere. Here, we were able to dump our holding tanks, fill our fresh water tank, buy diesel, and fill the generator gas tank. By now, we are realizing that no one just drives to Alaska. Most of the miles from where we started are in BC, and many will be in the Yukon and Northwest Territories as well. Good paved road greets us, and we read the names, initials, messages—all in rock—on the wide sandy slopes of the roadsides as we enter a Yukon plateau with lovely meandering curves and hills. There's another wide, clean swath of road alongside the highway. Is it there to widen the road in the future or as a fireguard?

Our warmest travelling day yet, then a patch of construction where the Highway from Hell takes on a new meaning. This is such a ripped-up place that for a fearful moment, John and I looked at each other, thinking we'd strayed off the detour and into the wild blue yonder. Then, thankfully, we saw a vehicle in the distance ahead. This wasn't construction. We were going to be learning a new word: Reconstruction! We learned that some of this new highway was actually on new ground, so the trees were ripped up, the roadway was cleared of bush, and when it was good enough to get a car over it, we were directed to do so. I believe I read that thirty-two curves were eliminated on the new highway because the original route followed waterways for convenience and less bridge building.

Onward to Whitehorse, with a sigh of relief, where a real DC-3 airplane is mounted as a weather vane, and a campground where the manager later took a vanful of us to see the sites in the area and spin some yarns of the days of the gold rush, including stories of his wife's grandmother who lived there in that era.

Forest fires were raging on our way to Dawson City, so we waited in Whitehorse and heard the big water bombers buzz overhead. We went to a wonderfully humorous variety stage show one evening and I laughed until my cheeks hurt. The comedy skit of "The Cremation of Sam McGee" was an unforgettable experience and I finally developed an interest in at least one man's poetry. The cabin of Robert Service was in the town and the next day I was able to go there to hear Tom Byrne do delightful recitations and talk about the life of Robert Service. For any of you who like that stuff, have you heard "Bessie's Boil"? I have it on tape and it sure is funny! Check it out!

By the next day, we were told we could be escorted through the hotspots of fire but were warned that the highway could be closed again at any moment as spot fires flared up here and there. The videos that we took going through a couple of those hotspots are the closest I ever want to get to a forest fire ever again. We felt the heat and saw the candling of new fires hopping from treetop to treetop right beside us! I can't say we weren't just a little bit scared, hoping the escort was safely leading all of us through and out of this danger!

In one area, there was a layer of white a few inches below topsoil that we could see along the cut banks of the ditches. Apparently this was volcanic ash from AD 700. We had *The Milepost* book with us and it gave us facts as old as that, and as current as where the construction areas would be, where camping and pull-outs were, where the biggest and best cinnamon buns were, restaurants where you could get the most delicious salmon dinners, and umpteen other valuable comments. A new edition is published each year, and we had the latest one through BCAA. It proved to be the best guide we could have wished for.

Jack and Muriel went on to Dawson City, and we went north on the Dempster Highway to Inuvik. When we had mentioned to my cousin Don Keller at home that we were going to Inuvik, he said his brother Ken has a daughter there. Well, I know we have a lot of relatives, but in Inuvik? Sure enough, Kirsten Keller is working with a dentist and they travel to the settlements from there. We didn't plan to do any side trips on the 456 miles of the Dempster Highway, so we left the car behind in a fenced area at a service station at the southern end of the Dempster.

It was 4:30 p.m. and usually that's time to quit for the day, but we were experiencing the wonderful "high" that comes with twenty-four-hour sunshine. There was no need to worry about getting to any certain spot before dark. There would be no setting sun for us for a few weeks. It sounds crazy to say it's sunny for twenty-four hours a day, and we know now that we really lucked out for the entire summer's weather. Boy, did we ever enjoy the sunshine. We learned that many summers are cool and rainy, not pleasant at all.

So, again, like two kids on a special adventure, we admired the monument and the dog sled on the top of the cairn at the south end of the Dempster Highway, and headed north over the spacious land of the Yukon. At 3,700 feet we expected to soon be above the tree line because we were so far north. It's such a vast land and soon our altimeter read 4,300 feet and we were travelling on slopes that looked like they were covered with a plush green blanket. We noticed many places where piles of rocks were stacked to form inukshuks. We climbed to 4,700 feet. We passed big patches of ice still on some small lakes, but we were wearing shorts and it was really warm. When the road widened and signs said "No Parking, No Stopping," we realized it was an emergency airstrip to be used as needed!

It's been pleasant cruising at forty-five to fifty kilometres per hour on dry lonely gravel roads, seeing rocky outcroppings and flat areas, making dust behind us and beginning to smell dust inside the bus too. At times, we were still surrounded by trees, and then we'd enter a clearing and have huge views on top of the world!

By 7:25 p.m. we were in bare-rock mountains. By 10:40 p.m. we thought we'd stop beside a creek in a campground surrounded by jagged mountains like castle tops. Big mistake! This was our first encounter with the vicious mosquitoes of the North! We hurried over to the registration box and back into the bus, where we were glad we were tired enough to sleep because we were prisoners in the bus unless we wanted to douse ourselves with repellent. There were a few other more hardy humans but we didn't go out to socialize.

We slept well during the bright night and the next morning the elevated road built on permafrost led us further and further north. There was no shortage of flowers on the tundra and among the bog plants. Some lookouts and stops had beautiful displays and were very informative about the area. Several times we felt "on top of the world" because we could see vast scenes of beauty that were so unexpected and awesome in size! The road snaked around another and another range of mountains. What a view— so many times! We never expected so many different mountain ranges. We'd get to a peak of a range and there in the distance was … another row of mountains to climb! We saw lots of areas of new and old forest fire damage. The wonderful weather we enjoyed was a big factor in the dust we were making and smelling and seeing. Really short trees now.

Eagle Plains is about halfway to Inuvik. There is a service station, campground, lovely motel, and restaurant. Engineers apparently saved many dollars in construction costs by designing these buildings to be built on bedrock instead of more expensive pilings in the permafrost. Alongside the road, beige-coloured hides were seen and later identified as caribou—hunted for meat, not skins. The gopher population liked playing chicken on the road, though I think they did win all the time. Soon there was a big pull-out and archway stating that we were at the Arctic Circle!

Another monumental moment for us! Stepping out to take pictures, the bog surrounding us was so colourful with the teeniest little flowers—but so many of them. As I stepped off the concrete pad, the bog was spongy under my feet, like being on the plushest carpet you could ever imagine. Of course, we had never experienced permafrost before, so it was all new to us. The road became more elevated and narrow after another milestone: crossing into the Northwest Territories! More pictures and excitement. At times, we felt speechless and inadequate to describe the view, so we just looked at each other quietly.

There are two cable ferry crossings; one at the Peel River and the other at the junction of the Mackenzie and the Arctic Red River. Caribou soup was on the menu at the food stand. There was certainly no problem taking a vehicle our size on the little ferries. The workers were so efficient that we boarded and drove off with expert guidance.

Entering North West Territories

Eventually there was pavement. We almost got out and kissed the road. A respite from the dust. The population of Inuvik is about 3,200 and a very active community. We chose the Happy Valley Campground in town because, without a car, we'd be walking a lot. We found the dental office Kirsten worked for, then strolled the town.

All the buildings are on stilts above the permafrost, the water and sewer utilities are enclosed in long, insulated above-ground boxes—also on stilts—called utilidors. There is a church shaped like an igloo, a covered pool and recreation facility, a general hospital, a college, a science research centre, hotels, stores, restaurants, art galleries, and several bed and breakfasts.

The busy, bustling town was a delightful surprise. After our walk we returned to our campground to go to sleep in the daylight. Up here the sun doesn't even get close to setting! As we were trying to sleep, we heard and saw kids and dogs, playing, riding, having fun well after midnight!

This was the Canada Day weekend. The next morning was July 1, 1995, our fourteenth day of this holiday. Last year, on Canada Day in 1994, we were driving the Cabot Trail in Nova Scotia, on the east coast. Now we are on our north coast. Wow, our dreams really are coming true!

We attended the big, noisy, and enthusiastic parade. Fire trucks were blaring and anything that could make noise was making noise, it seemed. Everyone was so happy! We started asking for Kirsten at the food stands at the hub of the activities. We found her boss, the dentist, wearing an apron and helping to make the cotton candy. He said he'd seen our note on the office door and would get the message to Kirsten who was due to return from a settlement trip that night. We meandered around town, arranged to go to a big car wash and clean the bus, then went to where the tug of war, log rolling, canoe races, and other holiday games were to be held.

We saw beautiful beaded slings being used for carrying babies. A woman I chatted with told me these beaded works were very expensive, and I could understand because of the intricate work. When we were in Texas, a fellow gave me some lessons in beadwork like the Navajos did, and I learned to make myself a few pairs of earrings and some dreamcatchers, so I really appreciated these examples of this skillful art.

During the afternoon I talked to an Indigenous man who said his name was Victor Stewart, the son of the guide who located the lost patrol of four RCMP officers in 1911. I mentioned that we would be stopping in Fort McPherson on our way back to see the historical gravesite of these RCMP and visit the tent and canvas factory there. When I mentioned my diary, he said I must meet his sister, Sarah Simon, in Fort McPherson. She has kept a diary of her life as a minister's wife. I said I'd like to try to find her.

The canoe races were very late starting, so we went home and by 7:00 p.m. the bus was at the car wash, and John was working hard again. The location was on a hillside overlooking the area of the canoe races, which finally were on, so I did get to see part of them. There was one team in particular trying so hard to paddle upstream but the current kept turning them around and they were carried back downstream so many times. We heard a lot of encouraging yelling and shouts for the teams, lots of laughing too. I walked down the hill for a while to be among the group, seeing those babies, enjoying their happiness around me.

We drove our clean bus back to the campground and relaxed. People from all over Canada and the US were our neighbours. We were surprised by the number of tourists there.

What a lovely visit we had when Kirsten and her pilot friend, Gerald Skocdopole, came to meet us! She said not many relatives come to see her there. We talked about the town, their jobs, our families, and too soon it was sleep time. The next day, Kirsten returned with Gerald's truck and gave us the grand tour of the area.

We saw the pastel-coloured houses, which make the dreariness of the winter a little less bleak, and the real plane weather vane, like in Whitehorse but smaller, swaying from side to side in the little breeze. It was a Reindeer Express aircraft.

Kirsten explained that the children often went to bush camps and fishing camps with grandparents during the summer holidays to learn to hunt and fish because their parents aren't doing that and are unable to teach their children. The diets of the youngsters are disastrous now that pop and chips are so available. Kirsten told us to look in the grocery stores at the tremendous shelf and floor space given over to supply the demand for these tempting new foods that are ruining the healthy lifestyle of so many young and old alike now.

She told us a lot about the towns. This one has a diesel-powered generating station, as do most, to supply the power. Fuel comes in huge tanks by barge in the summer from Yellowknife. Kirsten and Gerald should be writing books about their lives up north. It is truly amazing, and so different. She shared lots of tidbits about life here. When you are in Inuvik and you talk about going down south, you probably mean to Whitehorse. Planes are used like taxis. Sturdy duffel bags carry frozen meats and groceries from shopping trips down south. What a great tour guide she was.

Next morning was Sunday, by 8:00 a.m. we were parked at the auto clinic to have the oil bath air cleaner serviced. John was sure glad that was done because the oil was dirty! The young mechanic said it's the only place he knows where a mechanic can make $100,000 a year, if he's willing to work all day, every day. In the summer, it's tourists, and in the winter, it's keeping local vehicles running that fills in his time.

By 11:00 a.m. we were at Mass at the Igloo Church, on a really warm and, of course, sunny morning. A souvenir booklet of the church left us marvelling at the story of the builder, an architecturally talented missionary who designed a saucer-shaped foundation that worked perfectly on the permafrost, and young Eskimo artist, Mona Thrasher, a girl who'd lost her speech and hearing at a young age and completed all the beautiful paintings of the fourteen Stations of the Cross in about three months!

My Dad had told us, as kids, to make a wish in every new church you attended, and we are having so many wishes come true already. Now here we were, in Inuvik, planning to go to Tuktoyaktuk, and who would have believed we would be doing all this? We are enjoying all of this new life so much!

The Igloo Church in Inuvik.

141

The Western Arctic Regional Visitor Centre had beautiful displays of summer whaling camps, but these days the tents are not made of hides. They are a heavy white canvas with a Fort McPherson canvas decal sewn in the corner! While there, we got our certificates for driving the Dempster Highway, and another for crossing the Arctic Circle!

With Kirsten, we found the place to book our day tour to Tuktoyaktuk on the Arctic Ocean. There's no road to it in summer, and it's almost an hour's flight in a small plane. In winter, the road is the frozen river and transportation is by snowmobile.

Kirsten went to help a dental assistant friend to pack for her first solo trip with a dentist to a settlement. There is a lot of gear for her to take and there's no going back if something is forgotten. They often have to share a cabin with the nursing station, so if there's a medical emergency or evacuation, they could be wakened by that too. The midnight sun seems to encourage people to stay up much later than usual and then, of course, they sleep much later than normal, so the typical office hours, Kirsten said, could be 2:00 pm. to 2:00 am, and that would probably work out just fine for the patients.

We got a few groceries, noticed the cases of pop and chips, found a bank machine, checked our 1-800 number. We were so excited because our son Keith and Sandy were on their way from Vancouver to Alaska to meet us. Kirsten and Gerald came back to share stories with us. We are so lucky to have them to visit with and to learn from.

In the morning, a van picked us up at our campground and drove us to the airport, where we saw Gerald leave on his flight, then took off on our own noisy flight over the MacKenzie River Delta. We flew at only 500 to 1,000 feet, low enough to see the pingos—round mounds of heaving permafrost that grow larger every year—and the hills and tundra dotting the waterways to the Arctic Ocean. We spotted some beluga whales before we landed in

Tuk. No ice in sight. This is NOT the frozen north. It is hot and the mosquitoes are chasing us as we go from the plane to a waiting van with Gus as our tour guide.

Gus was a likeable Inuit guy who sounds like he's talking with a bit of a clenched jaw. He explained that the village looks like a ghost town because most people were still sleeping because they enjoy the midnight sun more at night than early in the day. He also answered our many questions and told us that the polar bears are there only in winter and, if they want the food set out for the dog teams, they'll kill the tied dogs for it.

With the long dark days of winter, and the white colour of the polar bears against the white snow, they can get dangerously close before they are seen. The school is now located right in town to keep the children from having too far to walk in the dim light of day. Gus was asked about whether polar bear meat was eaten. He said only some of the elders eat it now. It's a very strong smell, he tells us. Does he like muktuk? "Well, now, you know, since the pop and chips are here, we don't like to eat the muktuk like we used to."

Again, all buildings are on pilings and stilts to protect both the permafrost and the buildings themselves. There are no beautiful buildings. Almost all are box-shaped like construction trailers and are dull colours. The Tuk Inn Motel, where we had lunch, was another long box shape, but this one was painted a bright orange. Signs at the doorway said to remove all boots and shoes and was the floor ever clean! Cindy, from Saskatchewan, was the only worker there to serve all thirteen of us. She served us a grilled-cheese sandwich and homemade pie for about $11.95.

There were more tours than usual that day, so another bunch of people were the lucky ones to go to the home of a local and eat a typical meal. Those that went said it was a wonderful experience and delicious meal! Too bad for us that Tuk was so popular that day!

We were driven to a nice gravelly area at the edge of the Arctic Ocean, where we would be given another certificate if we stuck our toes in the Arctic. I went in with both feet and John with one, so we have "diplomas" for that too.

Tuk is a spread-out community following the curved edge of the bay and when we were given time to walk around town and visit the homes of some of the craftsmen, I promptly lost all sense of direction. But we did visit the homes of carvers of soapstone and antlers, sewers, beadcrafters, and also Christina Felix's parka factory. Everyone was so quietly friendly and gracious to us. I bought a tiny carving as my precious souvenir, and have video of being welcomed in one home and watched some sweet little girls playing with their handmade dolls, beautifully dressed in fur trimmed parkas.

Tuktoyaktuk.

By 3:00 p.m. we were back at the airport in Tuk, Gerald had returned, and was our co-pilot for the flight home to Inuvik. This time, we flew at about 5,600 feet and forest-fire smoke had really gotten heavier.

We relaxed a little before making a salmon supper for Kirsten and Gerald. We talked and talked until Kirsten was very tired and wanted to go home, so we said our goodbyes to them. The long weekend was over and they had to go back to work.

Kirsten Keller and her pilot boyfriend, Gerald Skocdopole.

Our next day was spent walking through stores and having our pictures taken beside a stuffed polar bear, a black bear, and in an igloo—all in an art gallery. The young painter working there was from Newfoundland! We are hearing more and more that it seems like anyone who wants to work in the north WILL find a job. Any and all trades seem to be needed, and if you will work at more than one trade, you can be very busy.

We quietly left town, almost sad, because it had been such a wonderful experience. We enjoyed those last few miles of pavement until we passed the airport, then resumed the dusty Dempster. Soon we were smelling dust again, and the forest-fire smoke was getting thicker. When we reached Fort McPherson, the canvas factory was closed, and the friendly girls at the VC (visitor centre) said we could park right there for the night.

I remembered to ask about Sarah Simon, Victor Stewart's sister, and was shown the building next door that is the "old folk's home" and was told I'd really enjoy talking to her and the other elders. I sure did. The next day, as she sat on her bed, Sarah Simon told me about breaking her hip three times and wanting to be in her own home—but not yet, her doctor says. She introduced me to some other elders there, all wearing beautifully beaded mukluks over their stockings. When I left, Sarah gave me a yarn key chain she'd made. She was so pleased to have had a visitor to talk with, and I was so pleased to have been that visitor and have that opportunity. When I came home, I wanted to make a gift for her, so I braided over a clothes hanger for tomorrow and went to bed tired in the bright daylight. The Anglican church and the graves of the RCMP lost patrol are on the lot beside us. It was Sarah Simon's father who guided Corporal Dempster to find the lost patrol.

We invited the info centre girls in for coffee, then we toured the canvas factory and bought a sturdy backpack. We learned a lot about Arctic travel gear, tents, and canvas for teepees. I bought the book that was written about Sarah Simon, for sale in the visitor's centre, then returned to see Sarah, gave her my gift, and had her autograph my book. She used her Order of Canada title alongside her signature, and as we turned the pages of the book, she told me the background stories of many of the pictures. The people, the wedding dresses she made, the games they played, being a minister's wife, meeting the men, such as Jean Chretien, who later became prime ministers, the work of preparing and preserving the foods, the hunting, the plentiful food, the clean grass to sit and play on before all the streets were made and those dirt roads became so dusty.

This lady is a marvellous historian and didn't know what her family did with her cases of diaries and books, but I sure hope they will be preserved and published one day soon. I knew John was anxious to travel, so I left Sarah Simon much sooner than I would have liked.

At Eagle Plains, we weren't hungry enough for the Eagle Burger recommended by Gerald, but we went in to see the crafts and artwork, and I had my picture taken beside a stuffed caribou. We checked for phone messages (none) but a sign said Inuvik was not long distance. I happened to have Kirsten's phone number handy, so we got to say another goodbye. We drove until evening and pulled over at a wide spot.

I'm tired and need a haircut. It's so dusty. Yesterday I thought my glasses were so dirty, but I took them off and there was still a brown haze. There is a thin layer of dust everywhere, including in the video camera. Will have to get it cleaned this year. We smell dust, we taste it, we feel it on everything. It's still hot outside so we usually have a glass of ice water between us to sip on, and even the glass looks dusty with our fingerprints.

There is so much dust on the road that we get used to slowing down to pass another vehicle in the dust. The few people who don't slow down are not appreciated, like a taxi (yes, even here) and a couple of truckers. We saw no wild animals except a bear, a few birds, and lots of gophers. We learn that the heaving of the melting spots of permafrost causes many trees to tilt in all directions, and the name given to these areas is the "drunken forest."

We enjoyed our favourite lookout spots on the rest of the return trip. Reunited with our car, John said he never realized how much he loves it. We arranged for changing the oil again and the air cleaner, now that we're finished with the long dusty gravel road. But it was worth every minute of it.

This time, we left the bus and took a day trip in the car to what remains of the silver mining towns of Mayo, Elsa, and Keno. If the price of silver would shoot up, these towns could be back in business, but there's only evidence of what used to be. The museums are a wonderful surprise. Very well done. It just seems like some of the museum pieces in the medical museum were part of my training years, and the household items were all too familiar from being used on the farm when I was a kid a few (?) years ago! The closest we got to an accident was seeing a motorhome on fire on the road ahead of us, blocking both lanes. The owner said he was from BC also, Cultus Lake, just beginning a four-week holiday. The couple who drove up behind us introduced themselves as John and Thelma from Michigan and, as we visited, we had no idea how soon and how often our paths would cross again.

On day twenty-one, we left the Klondike River Lodge ($12 a day at the bottom of the Dempster) after lots of conversation with fellow travellers, who were all so nice. I think the constant sunshine and warmth makes everyone feel their best. Got settled at Dawson City RV park and Shell Station for $14 a day. Now we try in earnest to get rid of the DEMPSTER DUST. Did laundry and hung it on lines under our awning. Vacuumed, dusted, swept, vacuumed both sides of the mattress, and oh, it was so nice to sleep on fresh line-dried sheets. Even had time to start to clean and rearrange some things in the bay because we're having company soon! Keith and Sandy will be leaving Vancouver tomorrow to meet us here, and deliver our mail.

Sunday morning Mass was a real treat. The priest is young, good-looking, has a wonderful singing voice, and a sense of humour. He acknowledged the visiting bishop, Father Tom Lobsinger, and his three nephews, introduced as Huey, Duey, and Louie. When the collection plate was about to be passed, Father Tim asked those who were lucky gambling at Diamond Tooth Gertie's to please be generous and added, "I hear you were pretty lucky last night, eh, Father Tom?"

Tours were well identified at the visitor reception area, so we toured old buildings, the Robert Service cabin, the Jack London cabin, and the big museum. We'll finish that tomorrow.

On Monday, we finished the museum tour and more in town. We heard the story and recitations by Tom Byrne of the life of

Robert Service and his poetry. Did I ever enjoy that! John rested in the car while I attended this. We also toured the Palace Grand where Klondike Kate worked, and drove out to a gold dredge for a tour. The dredge is like a giant water wheel, with seventy-two buckets—each about a third of the size of our car—that scoop up gravel from the creek beds, sluice it, and return the gravel in huge wormlike rows, completely relocating the creeks they are scooping up. The sound of these giant scoops was a steady irritating, grating noise heard all the way into Dawson City a few miles away, 24/7, during its operation. Our guide thought the city people would surely appreciate the quiet of a breakdown.

We went home for supper and there were John and Thelma of Michigan, parked near us. Because they didn't have a car, we asked them to come to Diamond Tooth Gertie's with us where we all enjoyed the shows and fun.

This time, we almost noticed dusk because the campground was surrounded by hills and the sun, though it didn't set, was behind the mountains for the night. One still could read without lights, but just did not see shadows. It's surprising how full the campgrounds are.

We decided on a guided tour at Bear Creek the next morning. This was the repair, reduce, reuse centre for the gold dredges, where the gold bars were molded. After lunch and a rest, we went for a walking tour of the town. We were fortunate to have a most sensitive tour guide telling us there were documents and shocking statistics in the visitor's centre and showing us some of the unpopular facts of Dawson City. Like the wagon wheels getting stuck in "feet thick" mud because the rains washed down the hillsides that were stripped bare of trees for fifteen miles around for wood to build cabins. I can still hear the emphasis she put on some words to help us imagine how messy it was.

Of course, there were no wild animals to hunt nearby for food then either, and gold mining was more profitable than gardening.

Peoples' lives were being lost by the score. Doctors who had come as stampeders for gold were beginning to realize the high death rate from illnesses meant serious trouble for the city. In one thirteen-month period there were ninety deaths among these young sturdy men seeking their fortunes in gold. There was no sanitation, so boardwalks were built to keep dry; the swampiness bred enough mosquitoes to drive one insane.

Eventually people began to bring gardening into fashion again, and to learn from the natives that fresh food was so necessary. Persistence and courage by those who began to see beyond the value of gold saved the town from total destruction.

This tour guide was the best we could wish for, and she walked us past Madam Ruby's where laundry was the front business and little shacks at the back kept the last legal brothel going until about 1961.

Examples of shims needed to keep buildings straight showed why the newer buildings are on stilts and not leaning at crazy angles like some of the abandoned buildings built directly on the permafrost. Driving home that evening, we recognized Father Tim officiating at a wedding or anniversary on the lawns of the old RCMP buildings.

It was time to do some more housework before our kids arrived. We cleaned out boxes under the couch, picked up photos, dropped off recycling, but in the evening we dressed up to go to the Palace Grand for the Gaslight Follies Show. A message from Keith said they'd make it here by tomorrow night. We drove to the Midnight Dome to see views that were so unlike any we thought we'd see.

July 13. Called Karen for her birthday at 7:30 am. Vacuumed some more, defrosted the fridge, and we were ready when Keith and Sandy arrived. They looked in great shape for all the miles they had made. We gave them the quick town tour and a ride up to the Midnight Dome to the top of a most gorgeous panoramic view of Dawson City, the mine dredgings, and all 360 degrees of the surroundings. It's the site of a big summer solstice party every June 22.

Keith and Sandy used the next day to tour by themselves. I baked two more batches of muffins, a lemon meringue pie, and scalloped oysters. We also met another bus couple, Cliff and Anne Mattice. They had lived in Camrose, and when John asked if they knew my parents, the Perkas, they said they were dear friends but lost track of them when Mom and Dad left the Camrose area and then saw the obituaries in the *Edmonton Journal*. When John told them I was their daughter, she came to see me and burst into tears of relief to find out what had happened and how they both died so close together. I was able to show her recent pictures of Mom and Dad and tell her they had a great retirement life in Langley, BC, for thirteen years after they sold the family farm at Round Hill and left Camrose and Alberta.

On Saturday, Keith and Sandy went out to have a nail puncture repaired in a tire and tour a little more, while we washed our car and vacuumed it. We were amused by three rather arrogant new neighbours with Florida license plates. I overheard one say that I'd have to move my car so they could move in. I came to the door and said, "I don't think so." The third friend arrived and saw where the sites were marked and said he thought I was right. The first two decided that they could be wrong but called the manager over to see where we had parked. I chuckled when the manager pointed out the painted lines that we were well within. Keith was delighted that I actually stood my ground against the two men. So was I, I had surprised myself again!

We finished the caribou burgers we bought in Inuvik and went to 7:00 p.m. Mass with Father Tim. He played the guitar, and the bearded miner was the Eucharistic minister with the wine. After Mass we toured the restoration taking place upstairs. Keith and Sandy asked at the VC which pub the locals go to. The Midnight Sun was one, so we shared a pitcher of beer there while pool was played. Arm wrestling and lots of beer drinking was going on. John commented to Keith that the guys doing the arm wrestling were a good example of good-natured fun that could turn into a brawl in a flash because of all the beer. We decided to try the Sourdough Saloon, but it was too touristy and quiet. "No atmosphere," we said. We walked a bit, visited a gallery that was open, and left Keith and Sandy to prowl more. We went home to phone Al and Jenny. When Keith and Sandy came back, they said that as they passed the Midnight Sun saloon later, someone was being thrown out of the bar! "Dad, you sure were right!" Keith said. We are still delighted with the real midnight sun.

By 10:30 a.m. on Sunday morning, we were all on the ferry leaving Dawson City and climbed the Top of the World Highway. To say we saw panoramic views and vistas would be an understatement. What we saw were scenes that went on forever! Forested valleys and rivers look so small from so far above. We climbed on good, dry roads without guard rails to about 4,500 feet and found a beautiful spot to have our lunch of sandwiches made with the rest of the caribou. It was like being on a ledge of the mountain, overlooking the universe.

The Top of the World Highway.

We crossed into Alaska at a tiny customs building and found a nice stop by a creek at Chicken, with lots of souvenirs, food, and gold panning, but we were told not to miss the real Chicken, a quarter mile in from the highway. Chicken is just a short street with an old log building housing a saloon with ball caps covering walls and ceilings, and the floor was very crooked. There was a souvenir shop and a restaurant where we had a bite to eat just to listen to the staff, who were a little different. Apparently, Chicken was named after the ptarmigans there, but that was too hard to spell.

From feeling on top of the world, we went on the American portion—the Taylor Highway—in a state of reconstruction so rough that most dug-up pastures would have been easier to drive on. We unhooked the car and drove separately, and could only be glad this was Sunday and the machines were at rest. Sometimes it seemed impossible to fit the car between the boulders on the road, much less the bus, but we made it again to pavement and to Tok. The visitor centre there had all the answers to our questions. They named the free parking and camping places we could choose from, and said this tour of the area would take about five minutes. They guided us to our requested sourdough pancakes and reindeer sausage. Campgrounds ranged from $18 to freebies and we were happy to choose from the latter. As Keith said, "Even beggars can be choosers here."

Day 30 already. Found the delicious sourdough pancakes and reindeer sausage breakfast. I bought a pound of reindeer sausage for $4.50. When we toured the gas and diesel stations, we found the one with the volume discount for diesel, a good gas price for the cars, and a free wash for all three! Sandy and I came back from a bank machine to find Cliff and Anne parked beside our bus! We are so recognizable that others can find us and we get to visit with them again like old friends.

John spent time hooking up the CB from our car to be in Keith's car for the ride to Fairbanks so we could chat to each other along the way. Keith and Sandy's CB name would be Top Dog because that's the name of the hot dog cart they own at home. It's their way to help earn enough to pay toward their student loans.

We navigated through some more construction where we had to unhook the car again to drive it separately. Soon after we were back on good pavement, we heard that sound of a shot again. Another inside dual skin. It's not the retreads that are at fault. It's the skins they were put on, said John. He grabbed the CB and called HOT DOG, HOT DOG, but Top Dog was out of range, and there was nothing we could do about it. We could have asked someone on the CB to help, but we were too shy.

It took more than two hours to get the tire changed at a shop with no equipment or familiarity with our size. I told John I had talked to Keith and Sandy about an emergency situation if we should have one, that the visitor centres would be our contact points. Our next stop would be North Pole, so they or a note should be there but it was too late for the centre to be open now. Lo and behold, when we arrived at the info centre at North Pole, there was a note with our name on it pinned to the door! Keith and Sandy left it when the office had to close and they would continue to the info centre in Fairbanks. So we carried on north toward Fairbanks. Keith came running out from a restaurant when he heard us drive up. He said they were waiting so long for us but had just ordered. It was about 9:00 p.m. and I sure didn't want to make a meal, so we asked them to move to a table for four, and we'd be in as soon as we unhooked and parked properly because this was the centre of town. What a reception when we came into the restaurant. The waiter said with an overly generously flourishing hand gesture, "Well, it's about time you got here. We were SO worried about you." We explained our flat tire and he kindly bought us each an iced tea.

We had great conversation that evening about how we eventually connected. We asked about where to park. Our waiter said we could join everyone else on the Sam's Club lot. So we did.

Keith and Sandy went sightseeing while we found a tire repair place, took the bus there for a replacement tire installation, then back to Sam's Club, took the car to the University of Fairbanks and happened to park right next to Keith and Sandy's car. We met them in the museum and they led us to the experimental farm for large animals—muskox, caribou, reindeer. They had already been there before they went to the museum.

As we left Fairbanks, we agreed that it's a really neat place with a great road system, and there was a lot to see if we could have spent more time there. We climbed out the valley from Fairbanks into views that just don't quit! Despite a few clouds, we had great weather and great roads, lots of tall birch trees and evergreens. Clouds increased as we entered Denali National Park and Preserve, toured the visitor centre, and booked an eight-hour safari ride for 2:30 pm. tomorrow. The kids went to a dog-sled demonstration. We drove to find a place to park the bus overnight. So many places were full and we had to settle for a $16 spot with no hookups! Expensive, but an amazing place. Returned to Denali and drove the fourteen miles into the park that the public is allowed in without a permit. Saw a cow moose. We met our kids again for the 6:00 p.m. movie and 7:00 p.m. presentation by a forest ranger who lives in a cabin without electricity about four miles in from the road.

We were very happy to get front seats on the safari bus the next morning, and videoed a lot of this ride. The long haired, bearded bus driver was a Gentle Ben kind of guy who loved this job that let him see the animals. We saw lots of caribou, Dall sheep, ptarmigan, moose, fox, a marmot, and twelve grizzlies—counting the cubs. We even saw one grizzly roll part way down a hill and my video camera got it! Our driver said his record was seeing fourteen grizzlies in one trip, so we sure saw our share! The road after the first fourteen miles became a one-lane strand just hanging on to the mountainside and we climbed and climbed and climbed. Rather than disturb an animal, our driver would shut off the engine to let the animal pass or cross undisturbed. We had a stop at Polychrome Pass that was another spectacular viewing area with a grizzly nearby and a supper stop among caribou at the end of our route. Very few people get to see the gigantic Mount McKinley. Clouds were in front and around it for us, but we were lucky to see the two peaks of the mountain well above the clouds.

As we returned toward Anchorage, I rode with Keith for a while and Sandy rode with John. Beautiful new roads and bright purple fireweed thick at the roadsides made for a smooth, colourful ride. Have I mentioned that in the years after a forest fire, the burned-out forest floor becomes covered with the fireweed plant, which has vivid reddish purple blooms carpeting the entire area? Such a lovely, consoling sight after the destruction of so much forest greenery.

We found a space to overnight on a mall lot in Eagle River. While it rained, Keith and Sandy went for a walk and I baked four dozen more bran muffins.

Came into Anchorage to Ship Creek Landings Campground. $25 US! And right beside a railway track! But a downtown location. We attended the farmers market, bought a few souvenirs, visited the uniquely gorgeous VC in a log-cabin building festooned by the biggest flowering baskets and pots of flowers everywhere! We toured the seawall, and Keith and Sandy walked part of it. We drove ahead to meet them, went sightseeing around the beautiful city, and walked all through Earthquake Park, commemorating the quake of 1964.

The huge hanging baskets in Anchorage.

The annual races of the Iditarod dog team begin in front of Blondie's restaurant, where we let the young ones treat us to salmon and halibut dinners. A fudge sundae and a banana split were shared for dessert. This was our last evening with them and we knew we would really miss them. The guys went out to see some small float planes while the girls did the laundry.

At 6:30 a.m., that first train sounded like it was coming right through the bus! Said our good-byes to Keith and Sandy in light rain, then we moved to the Walmart lot, and thought about Keith and Sandy driving for the next six days. I cooked a pot of chili and we watched a movie. We went to the 5:30 p.m. Mass after visiting the qiviut store. Qiviut is compared to angora, a warm, soft, woolly material the muskox sheds every spring. The knit garments are lighter, softer, and warmer than wool, and can be easily washed, but qiviut costs about $70 a ball! While driving around town, we admired the huge murals on some buildings, such as the

JCPenney store, and everywhere there were more huge, brightly coloured flowers. Such a lovely benefit of all the hours of sunshine.

Most dreary type of day with rain. Spent the morning finishing editing a video of Marc to send to Montréal. In the afternoon we went to the Alaska Experience, then to the Earthquake Show. We fueled up a propane tank, car gas, generator gas, and were amazed at the generator giving almost ten hours of service from one five-gallon tank. The temperature was cold, and dark-grey, low clouds hung in. We put extra blankets on our bed that night. Tourists from New York on one side of us, Arkansas on the other.

Another dreary, rainy, cold day, but we toured anyway. Saw a heritage cemetery where some grave markers were whale tusks, airplane propellers, artists' palettes, and other unusual shapes. Saw the Oscar Anderson House and the statue of Captain Cook, and went home to cook the second fish from Kirsten. Phoned our Alaska friends, Larry and Sandra Stangeland, and invited them to supper at the Fred Meyer parking lot tomorrow night. The place has been highly recommended.

It's warm sunshine again as we drive through more spectacular scenery along Turnagain Arm. Explorer James Cook thought he was heading to open waters years ago, but he came to the end and had to turn around. We saw glaciers, low grasslands, and dead spruce trees where the 1964 earthquake dropped the earth between six to twelve feet and salt water invaded the tree roots, killing them.

Today, we entered the Kenai Peninsula, Alaska's playground, as the signs tell us. Oh yes! No problem finding Fred Meyer's store, just a big problem believing what we were seeing! A campground on the paved parking lot … even a sani-dump and fresh water for the visitors!!!! The store, of course, sells everything—food, clothes, photo developing, fishing licenses and gear—everything you need. And, we recognized our Burnaby friends' bus, Andrew and Helen McLennan. We had hoped to meet them but they were travelling in the opposite direction. They had not yet been to Denali, Fairbanks, Dawson, Inuvik. We had a great reunion and then also with Larry and Sandra, Alaskans we met in Arizona (As long as we can get to a telephone, we can make all sorts of arrangements wherever we are.) A moose and her calves walked right beside the bush where Andrew and Helen were parked with their new friends, Ann and Al. They are all two-day-old "experts" at fishing and are canning their fresh catch already. Free advice and enthusiasm got John to drag out the tackle boxes we have carried without opening for four and a half years already. By evening, John was the proud owner of a fourteen-day fishing license, chest waders, and the alarm was set for 6 am.!! Go, John, go! Break your old record of never catching a fish!

John was up and out early, and I stayed in bed listening to the radio until I was ready to get up. Read the newspaper from yesterday as I drank coffee and had a lovely leisurely morning. Guys were home for lunch. Andy got Al started on his own first-ever fish canning session. A newspaper photographer came by then, took photos, and interviewed them to do a story on "parking lot camping" and why people would camp in a Fred Meyer parking lot.

The guys went fishing, Ann finished the canning. Helen and I went touring to the Soldotna VC, watched "combat fishing" where people line up almost shoulder to shoulder to fish on the river banks. We went out to the wildlife refuge VC and saw a fifty-five-minute video about the giant bears on Kodiak Island. (Before we knew much about Alaska's vastness, we wondered if we could spend time on Kodiak Island and the Aleutian Islands. We were short of time and money to do all that. Hah! Alaska is more than twice as big as Texas!!) We pooled our food for supper because I had made a lemon pie and we were together at our "house."

The days are getting shorter and we are further south. This is the second evening we used lights at about 11:30 pm. in about a month. We had made arrangements to go halibut fishing from

Homer Spit on Sunday, the six of us. Ann was very dubious about going.

The road to Homer was enclosed by trees a lot but some good peeks at the ocean would come into view, and then we saw the spectacular view of Homer and the five-mile-long strand of land that was the spit with glaciers across the water on huge mountain ranges. Our three rigs were parked side by side, one row away from the water, facing the ocean, with electricity!

God is indeed smiling on us again! Such a gorgeous view!

I baked more bran muffins. We confirmed our halibut fishing reservations. It's very windy and cold again. Ann is very nervous about going since the weather has really deteriorated, and she wanted to see the boat we'd be going in. We saw the boat and Captain Sonny Miller. He told us he didn't go out today because it was too windy. He said yesterday was summer and that was his fourth best trip in eighty-one this year. Oh dear!

Al volunteered to provide the salmon for supper, Ann and Helen thought I could whip up another lemon meringue pie. I made date squares instead. Ann and Al brought a baked salmon that melted in the mouth, and a jellied salad. Helen baked potatoes and had home-canned green beans, wine, and a white tablecloth. I brought a loaf of sourdough garlic bread, matrimonial cake, and a candle. What a feast! We all went to visit the resort building, walked on the beach, then watched Barbara Walters interview David Smith about his wife Susan and their two little boys she drowned.

Saw earmuffs worn yesterday, today a toque. It's not even the end of July! The forecast is for rain today, highs in the upper 50s Fahrenheit. That's pretty cold, alright. I'm just content to stay in and write this diary today and watch the tide go out. This area of Alaska to Anchorage has the great tidal changes of about 30 feet and we sure see the differences. The guys went to fish for a couple hours, then John came home to snooze before we went to 5:00 p.m. Mass. Our group gathered to play cards in the evening.

Up by 5:30 a.m. to go on our chartered fishing trip, but home by 6:30 a.m. because that was postponed due to bad weather. So, we crawled back into bed for a few hours more. Today is Andrew and Helen's forty-seventh anniversary. We all went to have a delicious tasty meal of halibut fish and chips before we all met again at the Sawlty Dawg Saloon for a celebratory drink.

Another shocking surprise when we returned to the bus was Irv and Nancy's bus parked beside us! (They are the ones who helped us name our Dragonfly.) We had a campfire and date squares on the beach for all of us.

July 31. Keith's birthday, but no time to phone. Repeated the 6 am. departure for the halibut charter place, and this time we went fishing. It was sunny and nice for the first part, but clouded over later. We were having a great time, halibut was being pulled in, smaller ones were thrown back. When I went down below deck to get the video camera, I heard the waves sloshing above my head, and my stomach suddenly got a very unfamiliar, unpleasant feeling and seemed to flip over. For the next several hours, I was the most undignified person on the boat as I rushed to the rail from wherever I was, no matter who else was there, and retched. John said later he was so worried I'd lose my teeth! Somehow that thought never occurred to me.

While in the midst of this terrible queasiness, my hook caught a fish! Now we had been told stories by Captain Sonny Miller about how a not-young woman brought up a big fish by herself, but I pulled mine up a ways and handed it over to someone saying I sure don't feel like being a hero today. Turns out that at thirty-two pounds, mine was the biggest fish, but I didn't bring it in all the way. Nor did I care at that time. Some pilot bread crackers let me enjoy the last few hours of the trip. Our captain said I was the happiest seasick person he had ever seen! I'll take that as a compliment. He said he once had a seasick lawyer on board who offered to buy the boat so he could demand that he be taken back to shore.

Our fish ranged from eighteen to thirty-two pounds, and each couple got about forty pounds of fillets to freeze. The young people working on the docks filleting the fish were adept at their jobs—a marvel of efficiency to watch. There was time taken for a group photo session and a souvenir picture for each couple of the day's catch on our boat. We left our fish to be vacuum packed and frozen tonight for pickup tomorrow. Phoned Karen, had a nice chat with her, and Keith was there so we could wish him a happy birthday, after all. Visited with Irv and Nancy. To bed by 11:00 p.m.—very tired.

What a catch for the day!

Such an awesome view here, and such a lovely feeling to be here. But we'll move to the Fishing Hole, where it's $5 instead of $19 a night. Saw a cruise ship slide by in front of us. Got settled at our new location. Irv and Nancy went on their halibut charter trip.

The guys were out fishing by 7:30 a.m. the next morning and two hours later, John came by with the first salmon he caught in about thirty years of trying! We were so proud of that! We went sightseeing with Andrew and Helen around the area, including

Anchor Point, the most westerly highway point. It was just a month ago that we were as far north as we could drive in Canada, and a year ago we were at the most easterly point of North America at Cape Spear, Newfoundland!!! Oh, the dreams we are realizing!

We visited the studio of Norman Lowell, a great painter who makes light and brightness look so real. There is a most beautiful flower garden, the old homestead cabin set up like a museum, as well as his beautiful log-building studio with such lovely works of his. While at the cabin, Helen said a mouthful when she sat on a carved chair, smiled, and softly said, "What a life."

We drove high above Homer, seeing castle-shaped buildings, log buildings, and some very unique gate posts and signs.

Helen and I got fishing licenses because the fish are jumping all over in the Fishing Hole. It is an almost enclosed, deep circular area that allows the tide to come in and out easily enough. All the motorhomes encircle the edge, facing the water, so what a view again! Helen and I started fishing with our new rods, reels, lines, and licenses, but we came in by 11:00 p.m. and had no fish. Boo hoo! And a light rain was starting.

Next morning John and Andrew went out to fish early. I enjoyed the rainy view through the windshield—of the fish, the fishermen, and even a sea otter just floating by, checking on everyone. I went back to bed to really sleep in. After Ann and Al left for Anchorage, the three of us in buses decided we would all leave Homer. Just a few miles later, Irv told us on the CB that Nancy couldn't leave. She wanted to stay and fish. They could find us some time later down the road. Okay. We understand.

Stopped for Chinese food at Ninilchik and found a guy in a taxi-dermist shop who told us more about the area here. It was settled by a group of ex-patriots who started this Russian Orthodox community about eighteen miles off the highway, over a very rough road. They tend to keep to themselves and their religion. Fishing, canning, and government subsidies keep them going, he said. We stopped at the old village site, now an historical town. One old house had Russian and Alaska native crafts that were such ornate and lovely things. How I would love to be turned loose with a credit card to buy gifts and souvenirs! The harbour was crammed full of boats because of a current fishing closure. We went to see the old Russian Orthodox church at the top of the hill, overlooking the scenic site of the town.

We continued to Kenai, parked in the Kmart lot, and went driving around there after supper. Saw the distant volcanic mountains of Iliamna and Redoubt, and the offshore oil wells, about a dozen of them. Our Alaskan friend, Sandra, says her son works on those rigs.

Andrew went to get a tooth fixed, and John and Thelma from Michigan drove up because they recognized Dragonfly again! Went with them to the VC and got lots of info about the local fishing spots. Said goodbye to Andrew and Helen and went fishing with John and Thelma. No luck. After a rest, at a later tide, still no fish.

Had a nice visit with John and Thelma before they went on, we went to the 5:00 p.m. Mass, and later saw Irv and Nancy when we returned to the Fred Meyer lot in Soldotna. How can anyone ever be lonely with so many friends around, old and new friends, even so far away from home?

Day 50 of the Alaska trip already! Larry and Sandra came to take Irv, Nancy, and us to their remote cabin on the Killey River. The guys drove on the rough Funny River Road, so the truck could be left closer to the cabin. Then they came by boat to pick us up, and we finished the trip in an ATV. Max, the gentle pit bull, was our guard dog. When we went to the outhouse, he sat at the door to warn us and scare away bears, if necessary. There were a lot of bears and moose nearby, we were told. Propane, kerosene, and candles were the only sources of power for the cabin. A generator provided power for the power tools, and a gas engine ran a little portable sawmill used to trim the logs that built their home. We were taken out to the nearby Kenai River and had a ball, catching fish and watching them be reeled in.

It's a plentiful salmon run. Sandra had a lovely dinner ready for us, and later lit the kerosene lamps for our visit. It's a large cabin, and we got to sleep in the loft. Irv and Nancy slept in the cabin that Larry and Sandra just moved out of. It's now a rental cabin for wilderness vacations and guided hunting and fishing trips.

The boys went fishing on the nearby Kenai River, and we tried to help Sandra can the fish. We brought our own little jars and were we ever pleased to get ten pints of canned fish each!

Larry gave us the two salmon he just caught, and cut them into fillets to freeze. After a very hearty brunch, we visited their son's cabin with its novel furnishings (it's gorgeous) and said goodbye to the people and the dogs—Max, Tank, Bucket, and the cats—Velcro, RV, Boots, Buddy. We returned to our car at Dot's Landing via ATV and boat, and back to "Uncle Fred's" lot. (That parking lot was immaculately clean. You would see a camper pick up any stray paper. It seemed like a nice way to show appreciation for the parking privilege. The only garbage found was where the staff came out to eat, and dropped their lunch garbage.)

Though our battery was dead back at the bus, we started the generator to build it up again and enjoyed a happy hour with Irv and Nancy, followed by fresh salmon fillets, butter lettuce salad from Sandy's garden, green beans, and mango and vanilla ice cream. Such a wonderful day. It's hard not to keep smiling, even if we've been having battery problems and they will need replacing soon.

Mailed some cards to our kids, and saw John and Thelma drive in as we were leaving Uncle Fred's. We thought we'd meet again in Valdez, and now we were headed to Seward. No place to stop and fish along the Russian River. Too many cars parked for us to maneuver the buses, but we found a nice pullout by the Kenai Princess Lodge, where we watched canoes and inflatables cross the little rapids in the Kenai River, while we had lunch and rested.

It was a warm sunny day, a REAL rarity in Seward, and WITHIN 20 minutes of parking, we were on an all-you-can-eat crab dinner cruise to see glaciers and puffins, delighting in Nancy's squeals of delight. I must admit I was so pleased to be able to see the puffins, too. They were smaller than we imagined them, but plentiful on the cliffs we cruised past. They beat their wings very rapidly as they fly their fat little bodies to and from their nests on the edge of the cliffs. We also saw large jellyfish and many beautiful coves and a marine park for boaters in Resurrection Bay. Bear Glacier is also so impressive. On some cliffs the common white murres were so loud and so concentrated that between them and their droppings, the cliff was entirely a bright white colour.

Back to the bus after that great dinner and cruise, we drank in the scenery again. Once more, we were parked facing the water, a park bench in front of us, and such a diversity of boats in our harbour. The cruise ships, Cunard's *Sagafjord* and the huge *Regent Rainbow*, came close enough for us to read their names. There was a huge working boat, inflatables, and smaller cruise boats like we were on—always something so interesting.

The morning was cold and rainy. We're glad we took yesterday's boat ride. We were told it was the fourth nice day that summer. Drove to Exit Glacier by car and passed "IdidaRide," where you could ride in a dog sled with wheels. The glacier was almost accessible but signs warned people to stay back in case a chunk fell. There sure are some very bright and very dark shades of blue in the crevasses, as well as some very dirty ridges of silt. Markers showed where the edges of the glacier had been in past years, and it has receded a lot in thirty years. It's hard to imagine that it is disappearing so quickly.

The rain was increasing and it was getting colder. We passed a café that advertised clam chowder and homemade lemon pie and that really appealed to me. I wanted to come back there the next day for lunch, so I said, "That's what we'll have for lunch tomorrow." Without batting an eye, John said something like, "Oh, don't bother, honey. You'd be up all night cooking." I didn't think it was as funny as the other three did, until they all burst out laughing at John's quick wit.

From there, we went to Fourth of July Creek, where there were really rocky and uneven sites for $8. Drove to Lowell Point Road, a narrow gravel road with one-lane bridges and expensive camping at the end! Saw fish caught everywhere, but we think the weather isn't nice enough for any but the most dedicated fishermen. Drove around town, found a place for Nancy to get a haircut (I had mine cut in Soldotna), and we spent a quiet evening enjoying the boat traffic. A knock on the door was Al, our halibut fishing buddy. They saw us come in and are parked just a ways down the beach, so I went over to say hello to Ann. They have their son and grandson visiting with them now. They've been here just a little while today and have caught two kings (chinook) already—just from shore!!

Awoke to a very windy day! John went to renew his fishing license. He was going to lay down and rest while I tried to catch a fish. Poor guy! I kept interrupting him as I lost four lures, but he was super patient with me. I FINALLY caught a fish, but by then John had fallen asleep so I laid it on the table beside a ruler, took a picture of it, cleaned it, and put it in the fridge. If he thought I really didn't catch one, he'd see the picture of it later. We all kept fishing until about 3:00 p.m., then left to go to Anchorage again, sad to be leaving the Kenai Peninsula and the astounding fishing. We settled on the other side of Walmart this time.

Wrote out more than a dozen more postcards and went into Walmart to mail them. When I heard the announcement for free makeovers at the cosmetics counter, I went for it! Nancy came by, had her makeover, too. They took before and after pictures of their work. Looking good, and no place special to go. Bought another dozen postcards, and after lunch we took Irv and Nancy to Earthquake Park. We also went to Lake Hood, the world's busiest float plane harbour, and did a little more touring and shopping, and then ate my salmon for supper. Will head toward Valdez tomorrow.

Free makeovers for Nancy and me.

Rained all night. Drove as far as Glenallen in fairly decent weather, with only a few miles of construction. We noticed more yellow on the leaves and got to 4,000 feet again, and saw fresh snow on some mountaintops. The road today had been very twisty and winding along the Matanuska River for miles of many steep climbs and descents. The drivers are very tired today. Stayed in a service station lot, tried our phone calls, unable to reach Karen again, but heard Marc's new song recorded on the call answer. Called my brother Ken and learned that my sister Lucy has a new van.

Sunday morning, light rain again. Learned there is a 10:00 a.m. Eucharistic service here at St. Francis Xavier Church. Sister Dee played the organ, wore slacks—casual and friendly. Onward with Irv and Nancy to Copper Center Lodge, where sourdough pancakes were waiting, but by the time we got there, we were too late for the breakfast menu, so we travelled a bit and made our own lunch beside the road. We saw more tundra, drunken forest, and for a while the clouds were really low so we couldn't see the mountains. Travelled alongside the silver ribbon that was the elevated pipeline going to Valdez port. Saw evidence of spruce beetle damage.

Our next stop was at the Worthington Glacier, yet another highlight. This glacier was very approachable if you walked down to its edge, which Nancy did. She came back just bursting with delight at having actually walked on a glacier. Her ecstatic face is documented in photographs for our memoirs.

As the berries are ripening, the warning signs are out to watch for bears. Apparently the greatest amount of snowfall in Alaska is in the pass south of Worthington Glacier, and are those snow markers ever high! Tall Bridal Veil Falls is worth stopping for. To reach Valdez means going through incredible scenery. We said that even if there was nothing to see at Valdez, getting there would suffice. But Valdez did not disappoint and we found John and Thelma again as we parked at the Eagle's Rest Campground in town. Drove around town, went to the VC, saw the earthquake movie depicting the damage here when it swamped the town. The present town has all been built since 1964, three miles away from the devastated area of the former town-site. Only a monument marks that site. Had a delicious halibut basket at the Alaska Halibut House, where there were seniors discounts for anyone over fifty-five. Even though I won't be fifty-five for a month yet, we all got the discount. Drove out to Allison Point to see the "Secret Fishing Hole" marked on our campground map.

Did some errands with John and Thelma, then around 2:00 p.m. the fishing story began. John and Thelma said yesterday they threw all their fish back because they had no room for them, so I said I'd clean all the fish anyone caught, and Thelma's John chuckled as he said, "That might be a lot." It sure was.

One really jumped at my feet and I was trying to kick it up the bank with my foot and push it up with my new rod. John couldn't figure out what in the heck I was doing, kicking and stabbing with my new fishing rod! We ended up putting that one back because it was only about twelve inches long. I caught and snagged fish like I was charmed!! Many broke free, and some were let go. One nice-sized fish that I didn't want to lose got yanked in so fast it flew into a bush behind me, and I laughed when I cleaned it later and found a leaf in its mouth! We all caught fish. John, Nancy, Irv, all got silvers (coho). My John's is the biggest. John and Thelma gave us ten, the four of us got twelve, and I had help at the fish cleaning table that night. Our host said most of what we got was past prime, and only the silvers were good now. But, gee, they looked real good to us, and that's what we caught, so we kept them. Another camper said they kept theirs like ours, and had just eaten their fish done in blackened redfish style and it was yummy! Well, I have that spice with me (and about thirty others too). Freezers are pretty full, and everybody's happy.

That German bus that sleeps and tours twenty-three people is parked beside us and they are a lively bunch of travellers, cooking and eating their meals outside.

German tourists ride and sleep in this bus.

Next day, John drove Thelma and John on a six-mile trip recommended by our hosts. They were lucky enough to see a wolverine in the back country. I drove Irv and Nancy on that road later (those two couples are not towing cars) and it was a rough but beautifully scenic area we saw behind the town. No wildlife sightings for us.

There is also an enormous wood carving of a face in front of the Prince William Sound College here in Valdez. Back to the Secret Fishing Hole. Today we specialize. We'll fish for silvers only. Rocks line the bay and make good chairs for fishing. We just climb up or down as the tide changes. Yesterday Irv slipped on a wet rock, but his clothes dried nicely in the warm sunshine.

John and Thelma got two twelve-pound silvers, Irv got an eleven-pound, Nancy got a twelve-pound. My John was really excited to get a fourteen-pound, then Nancy got a sixteen-pound beauty and really deflated his enthusiasm by beating him, so she's champion over all. Today I didn't catch a thing! Our freezer space now doesn't have space even for ice cubes.

The tour guide from that German bus group came to visit, gave us a taste of the fish and dill sauce they had for supper. He was given six silvers by someone he met. He and John had a great chat about their buses.

Day 60 on this trip already! Drove around town a little more with Irv and Nancy. Last chance to shop here. John got Nancy all excited when he said he found a puffin tree. There was a dry, dead tree with little carved puffins on the branches. Cute as can be! Inside, we saw a one-and-a-half hour video about pipeline construction, permafrost, and the animals in the area. John and Thelma were left behind to wait for mail, and we started our beautiful sunny drive back up through scenic Keystone Canyon, Thomson Pass, to Glenallen again, and back to Tok. Took our same free parking spot behind a motel. Some rain overnight.

Surprised to see Andrew and Helen in Tok the next day, back from Fairbanks, ready for the Top of the World Highway and Dawson City, where we had already been. We drove through patchy rough areas as we crossed back into Canada, but still have 1,229 miles to Dawson Creek, BC, so we are a long way from home yet. John is very surprised that we spent thirty-one busy days in Alaska. He thought we'd be out in about two weeks. My Alaska fishing license expires today. Boo hoo.

Lots of signs warn of bears in the area. The tundra is covered with ripe berries and it's now time for the bears to eat voraciously, before hibernation. We seem to be travelling a long time along the enormous Kluane Lake, and it seems like about 200 miles of construction. The visitor's centre at Burwash Landing is another must-see for its display inside as well as outside. The world's largest gold pan hangs there, and it's a beaut!

For days now, Nancy has been trying to reach an uncle, Jack Austad. She knows he is near Whitehorse, but she hasn't seen him in years, and is asking for help from the telephone operators because he has a different type of radio phone or mobile. She's being very determined! I think it was a call to an aunt who gave her instructions on how to find their place, so we parked our buses and went driving off the highway. We found their residence and began a delightful visit. We were invited to bring the buses in and stay there overnight, which we did. The family loves the remote life, and we were intrigued with the stories and adventures of Jack's life with a courageous group of individuals as a search-and-rescue technician in the Royal Canadian Air Force for many years. He could probably write volumes about his adventures. Their motto then and now is "That Others May Live."

We got to see a video of a polar expedition that he was on with Charles Kuralt years ago, making a documentary for TV. His wife Pat is an extremely accomplished homemaker inside and out, including building their guest house. Their two home-schooled children have such a variety of interests and hobbies, and they participate in sports in Whitehorse. We picked wild blueberries in their yard, and John caught a fish during his first-ever lesson in fly fishing from young Leif. It was an Arctic char and absolutely delicious, prepared for us by Pat. Finding this family was a highlight for all of us.

From there, we continued to Whitehorse. We decided to go to the other show in town, *The Canteen Show*. It was done as if it were a show for the troops in the Second World War, with all the old songs. Irv and another fellow were chosen from the audience to go on stage to learn to hula, and before Irv knew what happened, he had an apron-type garment slipped over his head that had a definite feminine shape in front, then a long messy black wig on his full head of short white hair, and was shown how to move his hands and swing his hips. Not good enough! He had to roll up his pant legs too. He was a good sport, but was an ugly girl, and we have the photos to prove it.

Irv is in blue on the right

John and I went to Sunday morning Mass before we left Whitehorse, then drove to Carcross. So many new flowers had bloomed since we first arrived there. There were brilliant yellows now contrasting with the beautiful green of Emerald Lake. Signs for burls for sale showed some of the unique crafts made from them. The Frontier Museum on the way also had a lot of great displays.

On our way to Skagway, we passed through a unique area, called Tormented Valley, like a moonscape almost. We didn't know our geography well enough to know we would be going south from Yukon, through BC, back into Alaska.

This is another rugged area, steep, with a lot of history about the gold rushers coming to Skagway by ship and then having to climb this steep pass with all their provisions—and now we travel so easily by car. Again, we are amazed at more very high snow markers.

Skagway is almost surrounded by mountains and glaciers. Cruise ships bring in loads of people, and tours wait for the passengers. The tours were by helicopter, bus, train, plane, or just walking around town. We read that Soapy Smith was a real-life con man who duped a lot of people out of money or gold, and there was a play about Soapy Smith that we thought we'd like to see. So, we got tickets and strolled around the pretty town. This time, it was John who was picked from the audience in the theatre. The girls sat him in a chair on stage, and as they stroked him, kissed him on the forehead, sat on his lap, and swung a leg over his shoulder, they sang "A Good Man Nowadays Is Hard To Find"!! And this time, Irv had the chance to laugh, while John squirmed (with pleasure, I'm sure). Outside, after the show, he proudly sported the big red lipstick kiss mark on his forehead!

Later, Irv and Nancy took a plane ride over the Chilkoot Pass and glaciers, and we drove inland to a couple of old town sites. On our drive back to our buses at Carcross, we saw a full rainbow as we crossed customs back into Canada once again.

Carcross to Watson Lake. Passed Tagish Lake, which looks like a very nice place to come back to when there's time for fly fishing. Heavy clouds, but very little moisture. Wow, what a place this Signpost Forest is! After the first Alaska Highway worker put up a sign showing the mileage to his home in Illinois, it has grown to more than 20,000 signs now. Definitely a forest of signs on signposts. Settled in a Watson Lake rest area for the night.

A nice drive to the Liard River Hot Springs area. A real treat, especially for Irv, was the coincidence of being where two US Army helicopters landed to fuel and have lunch. John and Irv learned that the choppers used about ninety gallons of fuel per hour and were going from Fairbanks to New Mexico, being taken out of military service. This had been just one of their pre-arranged fuel stops.

The Liard River Hot Springs.

175

Those Liard River Hot Springs were an absolute delight that afternoon, and again the next morning. The springs are different temperatures, one very hot, a couple of cooler ones, and all so clear and clean. They are free! I think everyone should take the opportunity to stop there.

Muncho Lake is another absolutely beautiful, huge lake! It looks so clear, so still, like a postcard view. Nearby we saw stone mountain sheep, red fox, caribou, bear.

To see the bears at Fort Nelson, we were directed to the dump. Saw nine bears there, one was carrying a big orange garbage bag into the bush, as if he was going home with his groceries. Drove another twenty miles further to a pullout. That day we enjoyed our fresh blueberry pie. Now, don't think I make a lot of pies! In a campground earlier on this trip, we befriended a French baker, and he made up a lovely batch of pastry that he portioned into individual crust sizes for me and I froze them. We have certainly met some beautiful people during the travels we've done!

As we visited during the evening in our bus, there was a thump on the side. "Oh my God, it's a bear!" Nancy gasped. It was looking in the window by the driver's seat, right behind where she was sitting! He had to be pretty tall for that! John's good judgment made him snap the door closed tightly and were we ever grateful, because the bear walked around the bus and if he'd gotten his paw in the partly opened door, I'd rather not think about that. Signs everywhere in the area warn not to feed the bears. "A Fed Bear is a Dead Bear" because if he bothers people, he's a danger, and he did come to us before he tried the litter barrels!

Then the bear went to the fifth wheel parked behind us. He sure must have scared the people in it, because as soon as the bear went over to pick in the litter barrels, the other people jumped into their truck and flew out of there! As the bear took out the bags of garbage, he wandered into the trees with them, then returned for more. He came back, bumping on our door and looking in that window and walked around our bus a couple more times. So, after filming a lot of this bear's activities—including him eventually upsetting the whole stand with the litter barrels—we sat in candlelight to see better outside.

We were rewarded with a view of the northern lights. Not brilliant colours, mind you, but bright-green dancing streaks in the sky, changing shape constantly. As John and Irv played crib, there was a thump on the door! It was the bear back again! This time he was standing up at the front of the bus looking into the windshield with big brown eyes and as we jumped up to see him we smelled the rankest, rottenest garbagey smell—oof, he was stinky!! The smell must have come in from the hole in the floor for the gas pedal but we felt very safe in our buses and eventually Irv and Nancy felt safe enough to go to their own bus, and we had a good night's sleep.

In the light of day we saw bear paw prints all over the sides of the bus and on the trunk and hood of the car. We were up before Irv and Nancy, so John decided to play a little joke on Irv. He went over to their bus and thumped hard on it, expecting to see Irv at the window but instead it was Nancy who woke up first. She said, "Irv, Irv! The bear is back … or else it's John!" and when she came to the window, there was John, just a-grinnin'. [A year or more later, there was an earth tremor in the Vancouver area. Apparently Nancy looked at Irv and said she wondered if it was the bear, or John again, or really an earthquake.]

We did some chores in Fort St. John—fuel, laundry, dump stations—and then said goodbye to our travel buddies. They were going to Edmonton directly, we were not. We continued on to see my cousin Al Boychuk in Farmington, near Dawson Creek. When we were kids, our farms were close together and our school years were also together but since we'd both left home, I probably hadn't seen Al five times, although his wife was a very good letter writer and we'd kept in touch with Christmas letters. From our nice parking spot there, we left the next day by car to do a loop tour of the WAC Bennett Dam, Hudson's Hope, and Chetwynd.

Was that ever interesting! We were about 500 feet underground in a bus touring the big dam. Again, we learned a lot that day. We went to Saturday evening Mass with Al. His wife was away at a conference while we were there.

On Sunday morning, we drove through Dawson Creek, BC, where Mile 0 of the Alaska Highway is marked, and into Alberta as far as Sangudo, to cousin Courtney's by 6:00 p.m. for supper. He and his wife, Gloria, surprised us by having my Uncle Tony Keller and Aunt Mary there from Edmonton, and we had a wonderful, musical Keller kind of visit. Saw Courtney's legacy for the town of Sangudo, a great piece of art. He designed a monolith that shows the summer solstice and incorporates rocks as a sundial. Courtney was to receive a plaque and award for this creation.

From Sangudo to Ardrossan. There, a gathering of some of my brothers and sisters met us at a supper at Dennis and Maureen's. Among them were more family—Rose, Tony, and Lucy.

In rapid succession, we saw Uncle Mike and Aunty Elizabeth, many cousins, Sister Elsie, had supper at Aunty Helen and Uncle Al Kucy's, with Elaine and Laurie, then hurried back to Rose and Tony's where Stan and Irene, Pat and Tammy all came for a little hello. They were short visits, and when I wondered why we had to rush, I realized the family is so big that we'd need a couple weeks to relax and see them all, and we'd been on the road a long time. Dennis worked on our CB antenna and convinced us to stay another day so he could do more, so Rose and I picked mushrooms to dehydrate.

We parked again in Camrose to see John's sister Ann, and some of her family. Called cousins Leo and Roman to come over. Next day was to Galahad and to visit with John's brother Frank, Doreen and family. Made blackened redfish for their supper. Doreen had just come home from cataract surgery.

We continued then to Strome by car to see John's sister Lena and Harold Hauser and some of their family. Back in Galahad that evening, Frank's daughter Carolyn called and announced her engagement.

A hot day for Mass in Galahad, then after Doreen's Sunday waffles and sausages, we left for Olds, where we settled on our parking spot at John's sister Isabelle Blatz's place. We no sooner got settled when a cousin, Ken Keller, Kirsten's dad from Calgary, happened to be driving by, and saw our bus there. His wife, Barb, and her parents came along. It was a pleasure to see them all, and to meet Barb's mother and her stepdad, who died just a few weeks after that visit.

More hot weather. To Calgary by car to see Uncle George and Aunt Marie in the morning, where we also saw Aunty Marie's sister Kay, whose company we had enjoyed in Arizona before. Also, we met the man Kay later married, when he came to call for her there. Such a lovely story about them. Apparently the two were childhood sweethearts, but somehow parents disapproved and circumstances prevented them from being together, so after fifty-two years, they met again at a funeral in their hometown. Both had lost their spouses, but not their friendship.

At John's sister Irene's place in Calgary, where we carried on with more family visiting before we left Olds and Alberta, headed through the Rockies in some rain. Spent some time in stopped traffic because of a major accident. A car had collided with a tour bus and the road was blocked for a while. Stayed at Coast to Coast Campground at Blind Bay on the Shuswap, happy to be back in BC.

On to Chilliwack to John's brother Jerry's place, where his family also has a parking spot for us and he has two other brothers and their wives we enjoy seeing. It is so nice to have these family parking spots always available to us in so many places, as we had provided for others over the years we lived in our Burnaby house.

The reason I included all this family diary here is to try to excuse us for seeming to rush our visits with family. Living in the bus and being so transportable means we can visit like we never could before, and for that we are so very grateful. But, there are still only twenty-four hours in a day, and only seven days in a week, and we want to see so many people and places while we live in the bus.

By now, we're very anxious to see our own family, and after eighty-two days on the road, it was very nice coming home to our parking spot in Cloverdale, the place that those special friends had given us the use of, in this quiet rural location for whenever we are "home," where our own phone connection is—whether we are there or not. We now can visit our families and friends for a couple of months before we prepare for another warm winter, after staying in BC for two winters in a row.

Marc enjoys our rural spot in Cloverdale, thanks to the Burns.

Marc loved to stay with us.

Marc loves to draw.

Our 1995 Thanksgiving was celebrated at Keith's in-laws, the Metcalfes' home. Always a happy place to gather!

By mid-November, we were heading south again—this time for a short trip to park Dragonfly in warmer climes. The first Joshua tree I see is when I know I'm where we should be, getting warmer for another winter. The areas were getting more familiar each time, through Las Vegas, Mesa, Apache Junction, Ann Baronet's home, my beautiful Picacho Peak campground, renewing friendships, getting reacquainted after what seemed like a long time. The intent was to get the bus settled and fly home for Christmas for happy reasons.

Marc was becoming quite the artist and welcomed us home with some of his drawings and sang "Crusty the Snowman" for us. What a delight he was! Christmas Eve was at brother Ken and Jo's, umpteen gifts piled up, and a lovely visit. The two Christmases before that included cancers, but not this one!

Christmas Day at Karen's was so much fun. Our family gathered there in her basement suite, and someone found a Santa suit which John wore to Marc's delight and ours too, for sure. John was a real Santa, even asked Marc to come on Grandpa's knee, but our gasps and giggles at this mistake didn't get noticed by Marc in his enthusiasm for Santa visiting his own house!!!!! Boxing Day was at Keith and Sandy's, and more visits and fun with Marc before we left for the warmer winter again.

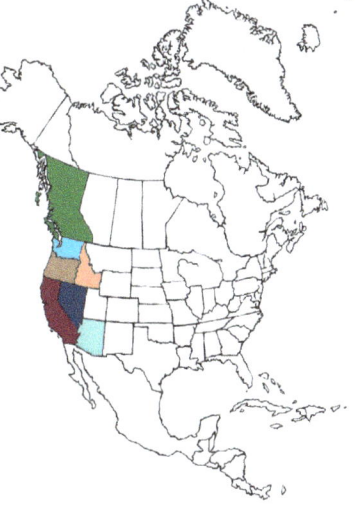

The Life of a Snowbird

After our Christmas holiday at home, we reunited with our bus and booked into Roger's Resort in Yuma for three months. There are so many things to do at these wonderful places, it's like a university for fun with a full class schedule of options without exams and with a lot of happy hours, crafts, hobbies, and entertainment galore. So much to keep everyone as busy as they want to be, and busier than they thought they could be.

We were so anticipating the visit of two of John's sisters, Ann, a widow from Camrose, and Sister Elsie, a nun, from Edmonton, for a January holiday. They had wondered if we were far from Disneyland and since we knew it would be their only chance to go there, we said, "We'll drive there, it's not that far." They arrived the second week of January and had to meet with so many cousins in the area first. We had found a nice trailer for them to rent for three weeks and have some privacy.

In a few days, we were off to Disneyland, enjoying the desert scenery all the way. The best times are remembered by showing someone Disneyland for the first time. Our kids loved it years ago, in the '70s, but they didn't seem to enjoy the long drive from home to get there in our truck and the camper we borrowed. When we took my mom and dad in the '80s, it was so cute because Dad kept running ahead, looking back to see that he could still see us and not get lost. Oh, it was such an honour to take them there.

Dad and Mom with us in Disneyland in the '80s.

And now, in the '90s, these girls, a little older than me but so surprised, their mouths open most of the time and such pleasure in their eyes. We had breakfast in our simple motel, took a shuttle to Disneyland, had lunch on the grounds, then supper at a restaurant near the motel, and had a fall-down-tired but happy feeling every day there.

We made a video copy for them to take home and relive the experience. I think it's time I watched it again myself.

John and his sisters, Elsie and Ann, in 1996.

Before we said goodbye to them, the sisters had tasted date shakes in Indio, toured a camel farm, visited a peanut patch, and found more cousins to see. Elsie thought she'd have time to relax and transfer her phone numbers into a new book, but she said she hadn't even started that and her time in Yuma was over too soon.

Our parking spot there had a lot of looky-loos; we felt the admiration people had for our bus. Until, one day a brand-new forty-five-foot bus parked right next to us!!! It was so much sleeker on the outside, had a fancier paint job, was higher than us, and five feet longer. Well, now we were chopped liver. People stood in front of our bus, admiring our new neighbour! We admired the new arrival too. We got to know them and visit with them, and found them to be a lovely couple. When they opened their bay door, instead of being stuffed with belongings like we had, they slid out a tray containing a stereo, TV, and bar.

As they showed us the interior, it sparkled with rope lights in the ceiling and along the floor, smelled of lovely leather, and when we marvelled, the owner said it was admittedly a little over the top, like a French whorehouse. Well, I've never been to one, so how would I know?

They didn't tow a car but an enclosed trailer from which they brought out matching motorcycles and a two-seater car. I don't even remember if I ever looked to see what kind of a car it was—I've never been car proud—just that they were in possession of much wealth.

They must have trusted us right away, because a couple days later, they gave us the keys to their bus, saying they were going into Mexico on a bike ride, and if they weren't back by a certain time, we should notify their son to start a helicopter search. We sure hoped they'd be back, but were proud of the confidence they had in us. They did come back and wanted to take us out to dinner to thank us—if we would drive, because theirs was only a two-passenger car. We did. We had a lovely evening with them. We met so many wonderful and memorable types of people.

Life comes in many flavours.

Various people visited and somehow connections worked and people found each other in the strangest ways sometimes. On one hot day, relief was in the air-conditioned clubhouse, where a couple from Nanaimo were saying how they wanted to travel like us for a while and had rented out their place. I said our son is in Nanaimo now, too. He's an engineer there. They asked his name, and when I said Allan Herle, they said "He's renting our place!" So now Al thinks I meet everyone in Yuma, and it's not quite true. We sure have met a lot of people though.

When we first met the Gleadles, our bus friends from home, Muriel said we would meet many different types of people but only a very few would stay close friends for years. That's proving to be so true!

During that time in Yuma, the Feldmans came to visit us from Tucson, with his sister May from Ontario. Lou and Nancy Taylor (my youngest brother Pat's in-laws from Edmonton) came to see us one afternoon, and also dear Uncle Martin and Aunty Yvette Madu from Edmonton came from their rental in downtown Yuma. Honestly, there just isn't as much time to visit when we are at home as there is when we are away, when everyone is so relaxed in these warm winter months.

The winter flies by, but memories will stay forever. I'm thinking of what I recall as the best happy hour ever, held in a friend's screen room, when the German Volk cousins and others got together. They told jokes in German, real knee slappers, then translated them for those of us who needed translation. There was accordion music, singsongs, animation like Bev Volk leading our songs by pretending she was the bouncing ball. Kahlua was enjoyed with other refreshments, and it was just one of the happiest, funniest, action-filled gathering and sharing of stories and songs that I was ever a part of that evening. There weren't that many of us inside the screen room but we would have been laughing so much and so loud that I have no idea how large an audience might have been listening outside that screen room and enjoying the infectious fun we were having. My cheeks hurt from laughing, and I wonder how many almost wet their pants with the bursts of laughter. I have that session on video also, thank heaven.

Also on tape are a hummingbird mom feeding her teeny tiny young ones in a tree outside George and Bev's unit. There are the sounds of mockingbirds who have quite a varied repertoire, and can even mimic a phone ringing. They can sing while they fly, exposing the white under their wings, letting me know those black birds are the lovely voices of the mockingbirds in spring, flying to the highest peak to sing some more, even on a TV antenna if there are no taller trees nearby.

(If I were younger and more capable with technology, there is enough material for quite a movie to compile from our VHS tapes.)

All too soon, it's the end of March and we start for home and taxes. Along the way we stop at many places to visit some more.

The summer flies by with more weddings, birthdays, fishing on Quadra Island or Telegraph Cove, many visits, and taking Marc with us camping at Beachwood, our CCC in Blaine, Washington, just across the border from our home base.

By November, we are southward bound again, hoping to miss the snow, even in the high mountain passes. So begins the next letter …

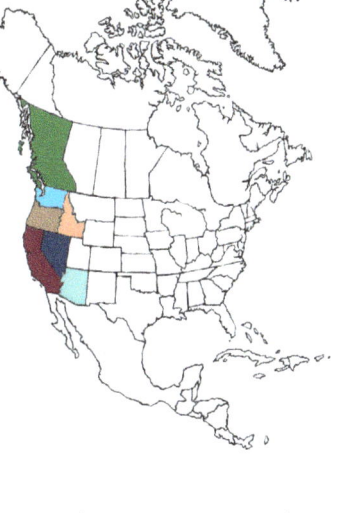

The Snowbird Life Continues

Dear family and friends,

Today is December 16. The sun is shining and we are in between Phoenix and Tucson at another beautiful Coast to Coast Campground, my favourite, at Picacho Peak for a week. That's some wild change from the record-breaking twenty-eight inches of snow in one day just before we left Chilliwack a month ago. John's brother, Frank, and his wife, Doreen, and their family were visiting from Alberta will never let us forget that snowfall.

The Herles, Jerry, Jack, John, George, Frank, and Hilda in November 1996.

Meanwhile, outside looked like this in Chilliwack, BC. A record snowfall.

The bus needs another apology for being in so much snow.

We really had no trouble all the way to the sunny climate, but boy, were the bus and car ever dirty when we got through the slush! John's been trying to wash them, but you know, so many friendly people stop to chat that it's going to take a little longer yet. And then there are so many other things to do. We went to our favourite RV store in Mesa last week and today John is installing heat strips in our air conditioner. I think that makes the air conditioner bisexual—it can provide heat or cold!

We've also renewed friendships with travelling buddies and John's cousins—those who live here and those who winter here. That's always a highlight of any visit to Arizona.

Then there are the activities that we just happen to be part of by being in the parks, like having our picture taken with Santa beside his decorated fire truck in Casa Grande, which Santa rode on into the park. Or hearing lovely music, or the local high school's Christmas program. Or posing by their Christmas tree.

When we got to Yuma, we were asked if we'd like to go to the Baja in Mexico. That's the trip that got cancelled when Mom and Dad were sick. Well, I guess we were asked in just the right way, by one of the other couples, Jack and Muriel Gleadle, who also had to cancel out that year due to her heart troubles. So, we said yes! We will spend the Christmas season with friends and relatives here, then by New Year's we should be in Mexico. Our destination may be only half way down, as far as Mulege. Our Alaskan friends, Larry and Sandra, had just gone down that far and were very content not to travel any further, so maybe we'll wait for a longer time on the Baja to go the rest of the way to Cabo San Lucas.

But no promises on how far south we'll go. We will return to Arizona in early February, in time to fly home to Vancouver to see our kids and reactivate our medical insurance because we took only ninety days insurance this time. We can fly home in the middle of our winter and still save money rather than getting six-month insurance at this time. We will be in Vancouver February

15–19, and return via Reno to Las Vegas where our car should be parked. Then we'll have another couple of months to stay.

The important thing for us to tell you is that we will probably be unreachable all the time we are in Mexico. If you want to find us any time, our kids will know approximately where we are.

(We will keep the Yuma Post Office box for as long as we're down here, probably as late as all of March, but after that we could be working our way back north. And it sure would be nice to get mail in February when we return from Mexico and before we go home again. I do plan to do some more travel newsletters but we just keep on going and doing things all along the way.

I took a sewing course to make sweat suits and T-shirts for Marc before we left Surrey, and now I want to make new curtains for the front of the bus. So, with reading and writing and sewing and crafts and travelling, I am kept very busy and John is busy doing as much as he wants to as well, and keeps up all the maintenance on the bus.)

By New Year's Eve, Mexican insurance, guide books, and Spanish lesson books were purchased and our next chapter gets written.

The Baja Peninsula, Mexico

Yet another once-in-a-lifetime trip begins …

So, as a group of four rigs, we left on New Year's Eve. None of us had any more pressing New Year's Eve engagement that could compare to this, so we left Yuma, Arizona, about 9:30 a.m., heading toward San Diego to cross into Mexico at Tecate.

A jovial young customs fellow let us all enter with a wave of his hand. Oh, boy, that was easy! He didn't see the need to stamp our entrance papers although we thought he should have. About one hour later we reached an RV park at Rancho Sordo Mudo, a school for the deaf and mute. We had full services there, and the opportunity to pick fresh oranges and lemons since we were southbound and there would be no agricultural inspections for a long time. Larry and Sandra brought beans, rice, and clothing that they donated to the school. We had a nice relaxing afternoon visit and had no qualms about going to bed very early on a New Year's Eve. This whole trip is a celebration to me!

New Year's Day was a short drive through Ensenada to La Bufadora, a blowhole on the Pacific. It was a very festive holiday atmosphere with lots of local people in the area. On the roadside were vendors from whom we bought our first tamales, drank coconut milk, and bought jars of home-preserved olives. Larry led us to a spot overlooking the ocean, where we parked and joined the throngs of people at the La Bufadora site. There were many other vendors there who tantalized our taste buds with fish tacos and a sugared crisp confection (churros),and our eyes were treated to the marvels of a happy festival. Back at our parking site, a man visited us and said this was his property and he would give us his written permission to stay there in case a "bad policeman" came and tried to charge us. Such graciousness so early in our trip!

Our group: Jack and Muriel, also bus owners from home, driving the one named *Flyin' High*; Larry and Sandra, our friends from Alaska, in their fifth wheel with Max, the dog, and their cats; Laurel, a spunky lady on her own in her motorhome; and us! Only Larry and Sandra had been there before. In fact, they had just returned from going halfway down the Baja, and loved the people so much, they said they'd go again and be our wagonmasters. What a deal! I don't have to worry about navigating for this trip at all! We get to follow someone with experience.

Our next stay was an RV park in nearby San Vincente Guerrero for 70 pesos—with free margaritas! There we watched TV and learned about the floods in Reno and the storms in Seattle and Victoria areas, and were glad we were where we were. Another sip of margarita, please.

We had been told about the things to expect that were different, and to have a few US $1 bills for the checkpoints we would encounter.

During the next weeks, there were stops by the *federales*—the army, agricultural department, drug enforcement—and never did we feel threatened by the usually young people wielding those big rifles. Also along the road, we were stopped by a person, sometimes in a uniform, asking for donations for the Red Cross, the ambulance service, an eye clinic, or for school fundraising. Donations were never demanded but the US dollar was graciously accepted at these "checkpoints" and we were detained for no longer than a rolling stop.

Soon we were in much more sparsely populated areas, amid rolling mountains, and the paved two-lane highway that goes 1,200 miles down to Cabo San Lucas through a variety of conditions. There are great stretches of new road where you can travel very comfortably and fast. But we had to be alert, as there could be a rock, hole, horse, cows, goats—anywhere, anytime. There are few fences. Some fences are made of datilillo tree posts, and for quite a stretch of miles, they rooted and grew as a living fence. Telephone or power posts were made of crooked sticks and branches, but they did the job. Some days we drove until lunch time, some days a little longer, but always being led by Larry and Sandra, and feeling very well cared for.

There are many plants endemic to Baja alone, as our guide book told us. That means they do not grow naturally anywhere else in the world. The cirio cactus is one of these, and it could be called a curious cactus, because it sure is different. It's tall and skinny. Could be thirty feet tall or more, with no branches, just oodles of tiny leaves that grow out of the trunk of the tree. Very intriguing.

The tall, tall and very unusual cirio cactus.

Larry, Laurel, Sandra, Muriel, Jack, John, and Max, our guardian

El Marmol is an abandoned onyx mine area about ten miles off the highway, on a very rough, dusty road. We drove about fifty minutes to make the ten miles! Huge blocks of beautiful onyx chunks are scattered over the landscape. A schoolhouse built of onyx blocks stands in ruin. A cemetery has onyx blocks and rocks covering the gravesites. The stones are browns, reds, whites, and have beautiful streaks in them. Apparently 5,000 people lived here at its peak, but the mining industry quit in the 1950s when plastics took over for easier manufacturing and cheaper products. What a loss! Makes me treasure the onyx souvenirs from years ago even more. We have onyx bookends, an ashtray, toothpick holder, chess sets. We parked for two free nights there, on top of a mesa, far from any other humans, and felt very comfortable.

What a wonderful time we spent there! If only our kids could have seen as all seven of us piled into Larry's extended cab truck, with the four-wheel drive engaged, as we rolled over the rocks and descended into that onyx canyon to be surprised with a bubbling spring where the onyx is created over eons. We found an area of white onyx that was exquisitely beautiful. All we could hear was our own noise. Such peace and adventure as we walked along cliffs of onyx and over smooth, worn rock on the canyon floor, finding weeds, flowers, reeds, and even cattails in the little pools in this dry desert area.

After happy hour in the schoolhouse ruins, we invited the others to a potluck supper in our place, and after a wonderful evening our company left and we noticed it was still just before six o'clock! Were we tired or what?! As we were driving away the next morning, I had such a feeling of awe and reverence for that place, realizing that we had seen a place that most people will never see or even know about.

Back to the highway and more rolling hills and boulders and bigger boulders and still bigger boulders.

Another such detour from the highway brought us to the little fishing village of Santa Rosalillita where we parked beside the ocean waves on a Sunday afternoon. The church bells began ringing and when I investigated, I found out Mass would be in ten minutes. I returned to the beach for John and we went to Sunday Mass, something I'd sort of given up for that day, being in such an isolated place. About a dozen friendly people, a priest who knew some English, and a dog guarding the door, all made our evening special.

Parked alongside the ocean.

So, the three couples who didn't get to go to the Baja the year that Mom and Dad were sick, are all now parked in a row here on the beach at Santa Rosalillita, Baja California, Mexico! We have spent only three nights here so far and have already eaten crab, lobster, and mussels. We have no telephone, no TV reception, no English. We have a gorgeous beach to ourselves, and delightful, shy townspeople who we are beginning to become familiar with as we enjoy the daily bounties of the sea that the fishermen bring in. Yesterday was such a cold and windy day with black clouds, but none of the terrible cold or floods that we have heard are currently happening north, especially in Washington, Oregon, Nevada, and California. I'm very sorry that's happening, but someone gets to be on the beach and watch the pelicans and seagulls, and I guess it's our turn.

Our four units were all lined up with our doors facing the ocean. While there, we picked from mussel beds and got lobster, crab, and fish from the friends Larry and Sandra had made just a couple weeks before. We traded the extra beef, ham, and chicken we were told to bring for this purpose. We were so content there, using sea water to wash dishes, boil lobster, clean fish, flush toilets, and for general use, preserving our tank of fresh water for drinking and cooking. The little concession-style store had fresh fruit, vine-ripened tomatoes, canned goods, other fresh veggies, Tetra Pak boxes of milk, and the staples we needed. Other friends, Bob and Donna, knew we'd be there and found and joined us for a couple days.

On one particular day, Larry needed propane for his freezer, so he and John left for the half-hour trip to the larger town ahead. While they were gone, Laurel and I went for a long walk on the beach and in the desert. I came back with shells shaped like parts of Dolly Parton. Laurel walks further than I do, so I came back alone. As I passed one home, a woman and two kids stood shyly at the door. I had seen them a couple of times before as I'd walked by, so I introduced myself and got invited inside to see her clean, sparsely furnished home. She gave me a beautiful large abalone shell from above her cupboard where she had a few more of those glistening shells lined up just like we display plates. I invited her to my place, and when she came she brought three lobsters with her. I gave her some ground beef, dates, raisins, and oranges when she left. In minutes, her children came running back, bringing fresh tortillas and a piece of frozen fish. We had lobster tortillas for lunch several times. We went for another long walk in the afternoon before Larry and John came back with no propane. *Mañana!*

One afternoon a young couple came into this town, needing some welding done. Well, there's no electricity in this village. Each home has a generator, solar panels, or a wind charger to make their own power. But yes, a local welder was available and he was most willing to do their work—but only after Mama finishes using the generator for doing the laundry. Then he can use it for the welder.

Another afternoon, a curious, well-mannered young boy came to see us. My limited Spanish helped me learn he was eleven and in Grade 5. He was fascinated by an airplane we had, built of ordinary aluminum soda cans with a propeller that would spin in the wind. I gave him a bunch of travel brochures and before we left there, we gave him the plane. He was spinning around, making the propeller turn as he ran home, very pleased with his gift. We left quite a few things in that little village and brought enough seafood and wonderful memories back with us from there. Jack and Muriel had been more anxious than us to continue, and felt confident enough to go on ahead to find the next mecca.

We knew we'd meet soon because there's only the one highway to travel on, and we had discussed places to stop. So they left, and the guys went again for propane. Later in the morning, three women and two girls stood outside, as if too shy to approach us. I was also too shy to approach the group. Sandra and Laurel said, "Come on, you know you want to," and started toward the women. I followed.

We all introduced ourselves and then wondered what to say next. (I'm learning Spanish from a book called Spanish in ten minutes a day, but I'm only on page 24!) By trying my limited Spanish we got braver and learned that two are sisters, the others a sister-in-law and two daughters. The sister and spouse of another were the school teachers. There were fifteen students up to Grade

6, and that's the extent of schooling for most children in Baja. The little building in the fenced area with the brightly painted tires was the kindergarten. The name of the church on the hill, where we attended Mass, was Mary, Star of the Sea. The little building with the funny things on it was the meteorological station, checked daily by another woman. We told them we'd planned to stay until Monday, but we left two days earlier because the trading of goods went so fast. The ladies or children would bring something and we'd give something. They'd come with more, we'd give more. Citrus, dates, raisins, canned foods, and meats—chicken, ham, moose from Alaska—were all traded for seafood. I showed the ladies how to make little gift boxes from used Christmas cards, then gave them little bead bells or soaps to put in them and more cards for them to make their own boxes. We had some straw Christmas ornaments from Algodones, Mexico, our border town near Yuma, but these ladies had never seen anything like them before, so I donated them also. One woman wanted to borrow our photo album that showed how we built the bus. She said her husband wanted to see it.

Another incident that makes me laugh was with a little girl whom I'd given some cheese singles to. I'd put them in a plastic grocery bag and she went away running, swinging the bag so hard it broke. I watched as she picked up the cheese slices, came back with the broken plastic bag and plopped the cheese back on the table, saying something that I could understand to be the *bolsa* (bag) broke. I gave her another one, put the cheese back in, and away she went. I guess the bag had to be whole too. When Larry and Sandra told them we had to leave the next day, all the boats went out early so we could have another day's catch before we left, with many hugs. Such beautiful people.

We had learned how to be very conservative with fresh water, able to have a complete "birdbath," shampoo included, in probably three quarts of water. In most towns, fresh water was cheap and available, but we learned to be very economical when we should be. So, by Saturday, we were in a city campground, could dump our tanks, shower, and found a 6:00 p.m. Mass, even made phone calls home.

How could there be a better parking spot?

Before we crossed to the Sea of Cortez side, there's a six-mile hill that sounded scary, but none of us had any trouble going down it. We were reunited with Jack and Muriel south of Mulege. They had found "the nearest place to heaven" on Santispac beach. We were just around the corner from them on an isolated beach, again over a very rough road. The beach vendors came to us with fresh tamales, blankets, ceramics, straw and ironwood items, fresh vegetables, fresh tortillas, and the catch of the day when the boats came in. We had such a wonderful feast of fresh shrimp for that afternoon's happy hour. Apparently 90 percent of the shrimp goes to Japan, so we felt lucky to get these!

No wonder we heard such wonderful raves about this area in the past few years. Watching the pelicans dive was so fascinating. They fly so low in formation over the water, then suddenly they're down for a fish and come up with the lump in their gullet that quickly disappears.

There's a fax machine in town so we faxed a letter home and were pleased to be able to let our families know we were fine. We met such a variety of people at the laundromat: a mature man who was cycling the Baja highway (must have nerves of steel and no brains), some adult hippy types just schmoozing and enjoying the sunny life in Mexico), and lots of others. We toured the town, and bought tacos and ice cream for lunch. The gossip was that officials were checking people on the beaches to see if tourist cards are stamped. Remember, the guy at Tecate just waved us in, so we were not stamped. So, we decided to go back to the nearest immigration office in Santa Rosalia the next day. We got stamped and fined 264 pesos each, about $100 Canadian. Darn it, but at least now we're legal.

Walked around the town and visited the church built of metal plates designed by Gustave Eiffel, who designed the Eiffel Tower. We found world-famous bread at Panadería El Boleo, and walked by the old, fancy wood homes with large verandas that were built by the French when copper mining made this a booming town. We made a couple little side trips on the way home, one to the Mulege airport, said to be the second-most useless airport in Mexico built by the government in its "wisdom." It's seldom used, guarded by the military, and is being used as barracks instead of offices for airlines. Not a very long runway, but a beautiful tarmac and excellent paved road in.

The day we left that isolated beach, I drove the car ahead of the bus on the two-mile, ten-minute drive back to the highway over those rocky, uneven roads. The cardon cacti are majestic and thick and the dirt and rock road are one lane with some wider places to pull out when one has to pass another. At one point, I looked in my rear-view mirror and will never forget the image—so sorry I didn't take my camera. There was Dragonfly coming along the one-lane narrow road—on both sides were cardon cacti one to two times taller than the bus and behind it was the blue water of Bahía Concepción (Bay of Conception). I'll never forget that view, and wish I would paint it and see it forever!

The majestic cardon cactus.

We reached Loreto and were four rigs again, headed for El Juncalito, a free beach where two other buses were, both from BC. We pulled up right against the high-water line on the beach and again were treated to hot tortillas and other fare from vendors on the beach. Such healthy food, and so fresh! It is so relaxing, I actually just sat and watched the waves for a while. It looked like the dark line of tide edge came pretty close to the bus, and sure enough, in the middle of the night, I could sit on the edge of the bed and look right down beside us to see the waves lapping!

205

Another amazing thing is the phosphorescence in the ocean waters. I had not heard of it or seen it before, but oh boy! As I looked down into that water, it looked like little fireflies or sparks throughout the water and bands of greenish neon-like glows on the waves as they'd break. It was so vivid and so weird! When I mentioned it the next day I learned about bioluminescence in the water and that it is especially bright after you see a red edge on the tide during the day. So every night after that, if we parked at a beach, I watched after dark and again when I'd wake during the night. I marvelled at this phenomenon and could understand better how people could see ghostly shapes on the water.

By now, it was our seventeenth day in Mexico, and lobster, tomato, lettuce, salsa, tortillas, and fresh fruit and watermelon were staples. Our diet was so healthy! This time Larry and Sandra and Laurel went ahead, and we wanted to stay another day to tour Loreto. Such a beautiful city, with its promenade along the beach, the old mission church, and the resort area of Nopolo. Nopolo had more *topos*, those notorious speed bumps, but here they were so big, our car scraped bottom with the four of us inside, so Jack and I would hop out while John and Muriel rode over those fiendish topos.

We left the beach the next day and, after climbing through majestic mountain scenery, we drove on a flatter area instead of going down the other side of the mountain. That's when I could understand the topography of the Baja as explained in the guide book. Imagine the Baja peninsula as a plank on a beach. Tilt the entire length of the plank. One side would be wet and sliding toward the water (the west side of the Baja), the other side would be above the water (the east side). Therefore, the Pacific side is much more level, and you really descend *muy rapido* (very quickly) from the east coast, which has a multitude of wonderful beaches below the cliffs. When you climb up from the east beaches to go to the Pacific side, there is no "other side" to the mountain. It's a slow slanted descent to the Pacific Ocean.

We reached Larry and Sandra on the CB as we entered Puerto Lopez Mateos, a whale-watching village forty kilometres off the main road, where we were to meet friends of Jack and Muriel's from Yuma. Imagine my surprise when those friends turned out to be Elaine, a lady I met in Yuma during my last haircut at another bus friend's place. We had also met her and Stan at a reception the past summer. Not only that, they live near us, in Fort Langley in the summer! Such surprises! Their little property in this village was big enough to put a bus on each side of their house and still have a fun time for two days in their backyard.

We attended a children's Mass on the Sunday, and enjoyed meeting Rueben's family—his wife, Vicki, daughters Uri and Wendy, and son Nestor. Canadian Stan and Mexican Rueben met and became friends when they worked together on a construction project in Loreto. When Stan visited Rueben's village, he bought the lot directly behind Rueben so they could share a backyard. Stan has been helping Rueben build his house, and now Rueben has the nicest bathroom in the entire village. A flush toilet and tiled walls and floor, while many houses still have dirt floors and yards that are dampened and swept each morning. They told us about the happy day Rueben burned the wooden outhouse seat on their bonfire.

In the evening, Rueben brought two big fish and cooked them over the fire the Mexican way and we feasted. We learned that Rueben has a boat and operates it for the whale-watching season, which is just beginning. He needed the letters repainted on his boat and that small job would take him a very long time. Jack is a sign painter, so said he would do it. Rueben was so surprised at such a wonderful offer. Jack said he could do a little picture too, so Rueben asked about a funny fish picture on it. The closest picture we could find in our limited supplies was on a video cover in Jack and Muriel's bus. We watched as Jack's steady hand painted the letters and numbers in a three-colour combination on the side of Rueben's boat. Now the little yellow blowfish on the video cover of *The Little Mermaid* graces the side of a whale-watching boat in Puerto Lopez Mateos. Jack couldn't have given a nicer gift.

As we sat around the campfire that evening, Stan told us of another evening when they had sat around burning scraps. At that time, Stan remembered something else to contribute: he went to his house and brought out an old pair of sneakers, laughing as he threw his worn runners into the campfire. But Rueben shocked Stan by immediately snatching them back out of the fire, explaining, "But the laces are still good!" That certainly made it very clear to us that shopping for those materials was not easy there!

We had a toy mechanical feathered parrot that repeats what you say to it, and Rueben's daughter Wendy played with it one day, sitting on the floor of our bus, clapping and singing to the parrot, laughing as it mimicked her and having so much fun. Just before we left there, little Wendy gave me a gift of an eggshell painted red with watercolours, glued onto a clamshell base painted in red, green, and yellow. (I still treasure that little gift twenty-five years later because of the memories that go with it. It was such a meaningful gift made out of what was available—just an eggshell and half a clam shell.)

At our next campground, near La Paz, Jack was the unlucky one to plug in first to a regular looking plug, but it was a sizzling 240 volts instead of 110. From then on, we checked first. His TV, VCR, and microwave blew, but he was smart enough to investigate and discover all three had fuses that could be replaced, which he did the next day.

Apparently thirty-six hours of heavy rain preceded our arrival, so all we saw was the beauty of the La Paz area from our cars, except for the little thatched-roof restaurant we chose on a beach, where we discovered the taste of their tortilla soup. It was so very delicious, with crisp tortilla pieces and fresh lime juice. Mmmmm.

Another wonderful incident was when Muriel needed a phone to call home. She'd been really concerned about a son-in-law's medical problem but we could only find the expensive type of pay phones, so we entered a little store and asked where there was the cheaper type of phone. Another customer spoke up and said his name was Moses, the owner of a nearby RV park where Muriel could use the phone in his office. He led us to his place, and Muriel phoned while we toured the little ceramic factory he had. Then he gave us a couple of hand-painted switch covers. We'll be sure to recommend his place to everyone. We all came away from there much happier.

We went for a long drive past the ferry terminal to the beach areas of Playa Tecolote, where a couple of roads were still flooded. Jack and Muriel met a couple from Germany who had been beside them at Santispac a few days earlier. We went back to the campground to hookup and continue on our way south. An older Mexican man bade us goodbye, wished us luck, and shook my hand. What a calloused, hard-working hand he had!

A short drive brought us through Todos Santos to El Cerillo. A beach campground again, with such beautiful, gigantic cardon cactus that dwarfed our vehicles. We found Larry, Sandra, and Laurel within easy walking distance from us. The next day, Jack and Muriel went ahead to Cabo San Lucas after we toured the picturesque little town of Todos Santos together. John and I will stay another day. Larry, Sandra, and Laurel will stay quite a while longer. It's their kind of place and great for Max and the cats. We met quite a few interesting people there, including a guy who introduced himself as Ali the Turk, his friend Wolfgang, and another guy named Lawrence, a shy recluse who painted desert scenes and had been dubbed Picasso the Fiasco.

In the morning, we drove through Cabo San Lucas to Brisa Del Mar, our resort on the beach at San Jose del Cabo, where we stayed for a week. There were Jack and Muriel! Jack had learned there would be a bonfire on the beach that evening, as there was on each full moon. John was engrossed in a book he'd just started, so I went without him. There sure were nice people there, and I learned about dipping roasted marshmallows into Kahlua before eating them. Mmmmm. During that evening, a lady came up to me and asked if I was Ken

Perka's sister! When I said yes, she said she'd been Ken's neighbour in Surrey and had met us there. How many more surprises!? They turned out to be ever so helpful in showing us around town—where to fax, get groceries, go to church, find the best taco stand, and more.

Jack and Muriel went ahead again, and we stayed to lap up the luxury of the area, and got royally toured through the Cabo area in the next few days with Dan and Lorraine. They treated us to a Sunday brunch at Tio Pablo's in Los Barillos where we ate on a patio beside a waterfall with hummingbirds flying all around. It was about a two-hour drive to get there, and we found Jack and Muriel on a beach on our way! On our way back, we stopped at a little zoo in Santiago that had quite a variety of animals and birds, but very cramped quarters for some.

One day, back at the resort, a parasailing boat flipped. No casualties, but the waves kept pounding the boat into the steep sides of the beach, and unsuccessful attempts by ONE truck pulling by a rope ended with TWO big tow trucks in the park finally pulling the battered boat out well after dark. Driving around Cabo San Lucas we saw luxury condos by the dozen, but there were much poorer conditions and dirt roads just off the main roads, and so many fabulous beaches with so few people on them. We are finally far enough south to put shorts on first thing in the morning and keep them on all evening too. Don't even need a sweater at night.

Another day, Dan and Lorraine drove us to the homes of the rich and famous on the Pedregal in Cabo, where million-dollar homes cling to the steep hillsides on both the Pacific and the Sea of Cortez sides, because this is the end of land for thousands of miles. We had a drink at the fancy Finisterra resort, lunch in town, and I bought a pretty, long dress! Then we went to the Giggling Marlin for a piña colada. When we returned, Bob and Donna came to visit! They had just seen Larry and Sandra, and found out where we were. We hadn't seen them since that little fishing village where they first found us. We talked them into staying for supper and a lovely evening as we celebrated her birthday! We had lobster, rice, broccoli, and the fresh chard we got in Todos Santos. Bob and Donna (from Alberta) look great and so tanned! This is not their first time on the Baja and they are travelling back roads in their camper truck.

John at the Giggling Marlin in Cabo San Lucas.

Thirty days after entering the Baja, we are turning around to return north. It's been great! Goodbye Cabo San Lucas, it's been wonderful! It was an easy day's drive to return to Puerto Lopez Mateos. But first, we had to stop and juice the sack of oranges we had with us because there would be an agriculture check at La Paz. We did our big sack in an hour with our high-speed electric juicer attachment. We made several litres of juice to freeze, but there was no place to put the peels in the garbage. I said I'd give them to the agriculture inspector. John said I couldn't. But I did. I was asked in Spanish if I had any *frutas* or vegetables. I told him I made *jugo de naranjas* and gave him the bag of peels. He said, "Todos?" I said, "Todos." He took our bag of the peels and disposed of it for us!

Juicing a big bag of oranges to get ready for agricultural inspection.

So, to Rueben's and Stan and Elaine's house again in Puerto Lopez Mateos. We parked beside their house and learned that Larry and Sandra and Laurel were on the beach there! I made a big pot of spaghetti for all and we got talked into staying another night so Rueben and Vicki could make a ceviche for us the next night from their big bag of scallops and clams. During the next day, we visited with the others, already on the beach, and bought fresh, warm, fragrant tamales from a young boy who carried them in a pail. We pooled together and all went whale watching to see the majestic and massive grey whales gliding so gracefully among our boats in the lagoon.

On our return to Rueben's house, we feasted on our marvellous seafood supper with Rueben and Vicki and their children, Uri, Nestor, and Wendy. We also revisited another family there, and another couple who would travel back with us tomorrow after we attended the market.

Next morning, we bought fresh produce, *queso* (cheese), and fresh tortillas before we loaded up six awestruck local youngsters for a bus ride out of town as we left. Stan followed with his truck to bring them home. Such is the trust everyone shows.

The other couple went as far as their place at Coco Beach. We continued just a little further to Santispac. Remember, there's only the one road down the Baja so you have to take the same road back, but what a pleasure to return to Santispac. We expected to see Jack and Muriel, but we were told they left that morning so we got their spot beside people we met the last time there.

Mass was at Mulege that Sunday. The poorbox was labelled CONTRIBUTIONS FOR NEEDED PEOPLE. We went for a drive, did housework, enjoyed the warm waters in the bay, and another great display of phosphorescence that night. During the campfire time, I waded into the water and splashed to make the phosphorus glow. During the night, John woke me up to see the lights of fish jumping and we could even see them just swimming. Another night, the whole beach edge was lit up. The neighbours said that recently some guys were out in their motorboats making donuts in the water to make a huge spray of light. So fascinating. Paid for two more nights.

What a wonderful world!

A castle-like structure nicknamed Pierre's Folly is being built nearby. It has many turrets and is surrounded by a rock wall and taking shape on a point of land. Apparently a Frenchman is doing this with only a thirty-year lease on the land. Oh, well, his money is employing many locals.

By February 5 we had reached the halfway point back to Guerrero Negro. We had stopped at Santa Rosalia where we unhooked the car and I drove into town to get some more pesos from the ATM. The inspection at the midpoint sure was funny to us. Army youth came in, asked us if we had drugs or armaments. I laughed and said no. They looked into the broom closet and then into all the bays outside. They seemed more curious about the construction of the bus than searching for anything. At a free parking spot beside a restaurant we met another two Canadian couples, one whose boat is called *Dragonfly*.

Again, I asked for flan in a restaurant, my favourite Mexican dessert, but it's not here today either. No flan yet on this trip!

The next day was windy and tough driving for John, but for me the views were spectacular! We'd go around curves, climbing at times, and at the top the view would be forever and we'd be on the crest of a mountain ridge looking down on both sides to other ridges and ranges in the distances, the bluish colour increasing on those furthest away. I actually gasped a couple of times at the magnificent and sudden changes of scenery. Again, we saw the miles of the cirio cacti, then the *cardonales,* the forest of cardon cacti, some gigantic! Another endemic plant is the elephant tree. I have pictures of these trees, which are very short with trunks thick like an elephant's leg. They have a whitish bark and can grow where there seems to be no nourishment such as on lava-rock beds. We saw them first at the onyx mine area.

This was a long day of driving and we found the recommended beach campground. By the time I drove in by car to check the campground and returned to John in the bus, we'd been joined by others, among them an arrogant Scotsman, who was an authority on EVERYTHING. John says he's sure glad to leave the corrupt government of Mexico. And he thought Canada was bad. We've seen so many government tourist facilities abandoned—some even before they opened.

Too many examples made us think of pure stupidity and government mismanagement. Same with Pemex. We drove 450 miles between fuel stops because we depended on the big stations instead of trying to squeeze into smaller ones, but one of the Pemex stations we fueled up at before was now out of fuel when we returned. Good thing we can easily go 600 miles between fill-ups. Smaller vehicles won't have that problem, but our size makes us have to look for spacious fuel stations. Some of the most beautiful ones were not open or didn't have the diesel-fuel islands open yet, and other big ones were abandoned.

An unusual sight at Catavina, in the boulders area, was a young girl, about twenty, sitting against a post on the side of the road. She was dressed like a hooker, playing with stuffed toys, drinking a large beer, playing with a tiny water pistol. Youngsters and adult locals stopped and chatted with her. Maybe she was simple, but no compliments to whoever dressed her in that tight top and flared miniskirt, torn black stockings, and glittery spike-heeled shoes. But she seemed happy, as did the people who stopped to greet her, so we shouldn't judge too quickly.

Back to the beach and the glittering glow of phosphorus again that night. Later in the morning, we went with buckets, bags, and money to greet the fish boats as they came in. We got about three pounds of crab from the catch of the day and our freezer is full of seafood only.

February 8, time to be closer to Yuma. A long day of driving through Ensenada, then a turn to the east, across the wide part of the Baja toward San Felipe, then north as the sun sets, and after about 300 miles of intense driving on very winding, curving roads, John was exhausted as we finally reached our last campground in Mexico.

We were within a couple hours of the US and glad to settle in after an unusually long day. After taking thirty-one days going south, we drove back in eight days, and maybe that was too much. John is saying he's going to be like the pope—he'll kiss the ground when he's back in the US. He's complaining about the roads—taking ten hours to go 500 kilometres. And he's comparing the Mexicans' living conditions to the conditions he already lived through fifty years ago—and didn't enjoy seeing this again. It is a curious mix—yes, these conditions are reminiscent of fifty years ago in Canada but jumbled with the modern here, with electricity and cars.

The majority of the people are poor by our standards, live in tiny houses, and have little money. Their interest rates are outrageously high so it's a pay-as-you-go life. Children all seem well cared for and happy, and bus service along the highway is very good between towns because few people will ever own cars. Honesty among the ordinary people seems everywhere and, if you ask me, it is a holiday I would repeat any time. The warmth, the

217

beaches, the seafood, the clean air, and the friendly people were so nice. There's so much more we saw, but I couldn't possibly write about everything.

We came through the narrow streets of Algodones, our very familiar border town, so near to Yuma, on a very busy Sunday morning, totally forgetting that Sunday is the biggest tourist shopping day of the week. The streets are full of vendors, booths, carts, people, but a very gracious elderly man saw us coming slowly, went ahead of us, clearing the streets enough for John to steer us through to US customs where we had no problem re-entering Arizona, back to the familiarity of Yuma. We parked and went to find friends.

Jack and Muriel were back safely, and after seeing them we left and went to another park to renew more friendships. Touched so many bases. Now John is giving his impression of the past six weeks and it made me think he was on a separate vacation from me because now he says his fingerprints are still in the steering wheel, and this was two trips in one to Baja—his first and his last. I'm so grateful to him for going on that trip, and he's so grateful it's done. There sure were a lot of motorhomes of all sizes on the Baja, and most were from BC.

Another dream trip accomplished!

More Bucket List Checked Off

Written for this book, not a part of the newsletters:

There are a couple more stops that would have been on my bucket list if I had known about them before we travelled. They are both on our way home, going north of Phoenix.

We had a CCC at Verde Valley and from there took a day trip to Arcosanti, an ambitious community-living development project highlighting the desert lifestyle. The project has a very small footprint compared to multiple single-family dwellings that use up so much land area for so few people, which is everyone's expectations in small towns and rural areas. Instead of using so much landscape for a single-family dwelling, they have grand plans for very, very tall buildings that would house huge populations, including their workspace as well as parks and recreation spaces, on a smaller footprint of land.

Terraced gardens, slanted to benefit from maximum sunshine, use and reuse water as it travels down through rows of gardens. The premise is a combination of architecture and ecology called arcology. It has been established for just a few decades and can earn university credits for scholars who come to work in this endeavour. It is a fascinating idea, and I wonder how it has advanced in these last twenty-five years since our visit. They grew food to feed their staff and small restaurant. A large amphitheatre was almost finished at the time and the enthusiasm was very pervasive as we took the tour. So sorry we were never able to make a return trip.

Another gem in our world is the Amargosa Opera House in Death Valley Junction, where California meets Nevada. What a surprise there! It had been difficult to arrange tickets for a few years to match a time when the dates for the show would coincide with when we would be near. You wouldn't think it should be so difficult to arrange, but our retirement was so busy, it was often impossibly hard to do all we want.

Well, I'd heard the story about this young ballerina, Marta Becket, who was travelling through this desert area from LA back to NYC, had a flat tire, and stopped at the service station here for a repair. In her wanderings while the tire change was being done, she saw this abandoned town hall that was a part of a rundown abandoned group of buildings in a U shape. The town hall at the end of the row of buildings was leaky, dusty, and so neglected but peeking through the space in the door, she saw a stage at the back. It excited her and she thought it might be a great place for her to perform. She was already a ballerina, an artist, could sew costumes, could choreograph her own shows, and could write new ones. She had experience in all those fields during her career in New York City. Soon she arranged to leave NYC and began renting the old Pacific Borax townsite.

It was a deserted place and not many people came to her performances, but she wanted an audience and eventually painted them on the entire back wall, depicting the interior of a sixteenth-century opera theatre house in Europe. She continued her stage shows and, over the years, continued to paint full murals on the other walls as well. With so much artwork invested, she eventually bought the entire group of buildings, making just a few rooms available as a hotel with simple amenities with some of her beautiful paintings on the walls there too. Then she saw that the ceiling could use painting also, so that was done as well, creating a majestic opera house interior in the dusty desert. I had read about her during our travels, and was determined to do my best to get there.

Finally, we managed to buy tickets over the phone during our trip home, reserving our place in the theatre, and drove there early in the daytime so we could ramble around, seeing the minimal furnishings with no air conditioning but a chance to stay in a historic hotel. There was only one couple as guests at the time, so we chatted with them and a couple of staff and told them how excited we were to finally make this happen for us. There was a guest book for us to sign, and the comments in it were very interesting and from so many different places.

I had heard the story of how Marta Becket danced at 8:15 pm. for each performance. One day, a reporter from the *National Geographic* came to investigate this place, but was a bit late for the performance and, as he walked in, he saw that there was no one else in the room but Marta, dancing alone on the stage, as if all the chairs were full. Needless to say, he went away very impressed.

We had parked our bus in the overnight campground, just an empty sandy desert lot with a tin can nailed to a power pole to put your $2 in for each night. Holy moley, that sure was affordable. Since this was the opera house, I thought I should wear a nice long dress, the one I bought from the recent trip to Cabo. John cleaned up pretty good too. It was after 7:30 pm, and no one else was there but the couple who had come from the hotel part and were standing near the front door, so we joined them and just chatted. It was almost 8:00 p.m., when the front door would open. I was disappointed for Marta that there were so few of us.

Then the buses arrived and disgorged many, many people who joined us in front of the locked doors. When a man in a top hat came to open the doors, he called out some names, including John and I and the couple from the hotel! He led us to the front row seats and the general crowd was seated after us. I was so happy to be there at last, but now I felt like royalty! I knew this was going to be good. And it was. The man in the top hat was Tom Willett, Marta's partner on stage for some of the acts.

The whole show had beauty, grace, silliness with so much talent and fun. And seeing the fabulous paintings on the walls and ceiling made me totally forget there was desert just outside the door. But inside the old building, I felt like I was truly in an Old World European setting, among kings and queens, courtiers, knights and ladies, counts and princes, with cherubs and angels overhead. I took some lovely video of her performing. I have Marta's autograph on a postcard photo of her, and it means more to me than to anyone else, I'm sure, because I finally managed to meet that delightful lady who was already in her 70s, still dancing on pointe and giving everyone the best of herself in each performance. That was an amazing gift to me, from me, with John's help.

Life is so amazing.

On our way home, we knew our family was fine and our grandchildren's count would double as we got ready to greet our second one. Keith and Sandy's baby was due in March, so I got busy with some knitting.

When we're home, we try to spend as much time as we can with Marc, taking him camping or just to wherever we were, and sharing time with all our family. Time flew when we were home! We entertained a lot at our spacious site in Cloverdale, even watched our landlord and friend, Frank Burm, help birth a calf one day while we had Marc with us.

We also spent a lot of time at Beachwood with Marc, enjoyed celebrating John's birthday and Mother's Day in May, Father's Day and Al's birthday in June, Karen's and Keith's birthdays in July, fishing with Rose and Tony again on Quadra Island in August, a surprise fiftieth anniversary for the Gleadles in September before my birthday, Halloween, Thanksgiving, then we went south once more, stopping in Desert Hot Springs, California, for a while.

Soon we were back at the Sun Vista Resort in Yuma, Arizona, for another warm winter. There I saw a notice asking for those who liked to sing and could read music, to join the Treble Clef group. I hadn't been in a choir for so long and I loved to sing. I can't read music, but I can learn quickly to follow notes, so I joined. Our uniform was black pants, white blouse, and a large, red-sequinned treble-clef badge. The choir leader was Mildred, from the university in Albuquerque, New Mexico. What a delight she was. We made beautiful music and sang "His Name Is Wonderful" and "Ten Thousand Angels" for a Sunday church service. I'd never heard those hymns before but oh, they were heavenly! I thought Mildred made us sound like angels. There were several other contemporary songs like "Mr. Sandman," "Santa Baby," and such that we sang at a different special performance in the park.

The Treble Clef ladies.

My uniform as a Treble Clef.

I also joined the kitchen band using some outrageous musical instruments. I had a whistle with water in it to tweet like a bird for "Let's All Sing Like the Birdies Sing." We dressed in ridiculous costumes and had so much fun!

I'm second from the right.

Three new friends of the kitchen band.

John said he had now done all the big trips that he intended to do, and our bus had served us very well. He said that maybe it was time to find a new owner for it, so someone else can fulfill their dream, and we'd move on to the next step. He thought it was better for him to sell the bus while he was still well, and not leave that for me to do. He was the only one who could describe all the features that were put into this home of ours. So, we went home to look for a house with an address instead of wheels.

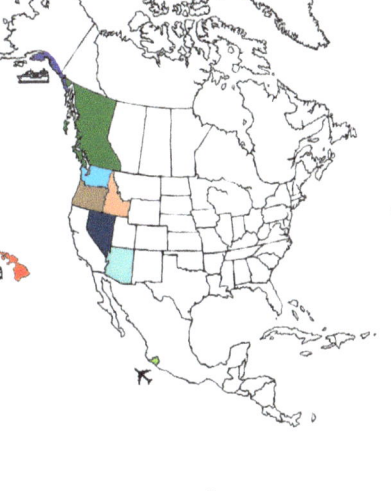

Finale

Last newsletter

It's time to pass on our new address and phone number to everyone, which can be written in ink now after exactly seven wonderful years of living in Dragonfly. We are homeowners once again and the bus is for sale. The big trips have been done. Now that we don't have to take everything with us anymore, we can trade the big bus for a much smaller motorhome—that would be easier for me to sell if I had to do it alone—for much shorter trips.

John's heart health was making us think that we should have a home base, so we found this little rancher in a gated community in the South Surrey/White Rock area, and are just fourteen blocks north of Washington State. It's been a real challenge to try to accommodate all the "stuff" we have stored in boxes. Eventually we'll get through unpacking and try to weed out a lot of what we don't need anymore. Our goal is to store nothing in the crawl space, and furnish a two-bedroom house tastefully with only what we can use. Most rooms are okay, but that second bedroom is still choked with boxes and "stuff."

The biggest change in living in a house after seven years in the bus is the waste of water in a house. The shower runs full blast all the time and a whole lot of water is used to wash dishes in the big sink or in the dishwasher, and just to flush a toilet.

But now I can do smaller loads of laundry, we can invite people over in any kind of weather, and we don't have to be outside if we have more than six people.

Our first granddaughter, Samantha, March 1998

We now have a darling granddaughter, Samantha Rose, born to Keith and Sandy in March and we babysit her every second Wednesday at least. She's even had her first sleepover with us already! What a joy she is!! Our Marc is seven, and he is a gem of lively imagination and conversation—whenever we can get his undivided attention. Last Saturday, we had both grandchildren for the evening and enjoyed them immensely.

There is a small yard to look after here and we have been so slow about working at our new place. We're too busy having fun, visiting friends, and getting to know the area. We accumulated almost all the furniture we need again and it's all very different from what we had seven years ago. Only a little TV and the little freezer came from the bus. We started out in our house using our patio chairs in the kitchen and living room and we didn't mind a bit.

Because the bus is still ours, there is a distinct chance we may put the bare essentials back in it and go south to Yuma again this winter. John isn't the least bit sorry it didn't sell yet, so he might have the opportunity to be warm in winter again in Arizona for a while.

In 2003, Karen married Charles, giving us two more beautiful granddaughters, and Marc has sisters now in a happy family. They are so wonderful to see together.

So, now we have our permanent phone number in the house, and our address is stable, our welcome mat is always out, unless we take a little trip now and then, so come and visit!

I'd love to tell you more, but just know that if you really want to do something, make it happen. If you can do at least some of your goals in your 60s, then your 70s and 80s are bonus years. Do the big things while you can.

John and I said we could always sit in our rocking chairs with our memories when we couldn't travel any more. I do have a rocking chair but I'm not rooted in it just yet. I'm enjoying my bonus years.

Some friends definitely thought we were crazy to do what we did, but for us it was the BEST decision we could have made for ourselves. No regrets.

Remember, when these newsletters were written, there were still pay phones only, no cell phones, no computers, no emails. We relied on a telephone messaging service, prepaid calling cards, and the postal services.

Fast forward … After selling the bus, we couldn't stop travelling "cold turkey" so we bought a smaller motorhome for shorter trips for a few more warm winters, and finally got to see the Grand Canyon! Usually there was too much snow, and John was so determined to avoid snow as much as possible. On our last trip, as we drove by car only, we learned that winter conditions were minimal in the ski area of Flagstaff and surroundings. We used a coupon book to get an $18-a-night motel in Williams, just south of the entrance to the Grand Canyon. We booked it and drove as fast as we could in the morning to the most eastern lookout, then meandered all day toward the west, from lookout to lookout, at last seeing another wonder of the world. The river looks so tiny way down below, and we were there to look—not to hike or do anything too strenuous or adventuresome—content just to see, feel, and remember what we were seeing.

When travel wasn't as easy any more, we took a couple of cruises where we couldn't have driven … first to Hawaii in September 2005, celebrating my sixty-fifth birthday as well as our forty-third anniversary. The next cruise was a summer trip to Alaska, seeing the ever-so-scenic coastline, towns, cities, and glaciers we could not see by road. What a difference it was to cruise, being cared for by the chefs and cabin crew on a ship. We did no cooking, no cleaning, no navigating! We were so ready for that! By then, John was using a cane, getting used to the idea of needing it for balance and support.

He continued to feel less mobile, and was really worried that he would barely be able to attend Al's wedding to Laura in September 2007, but he made it. That same month his vision deteriorated and a brain tumour was discovered. With surgery, it was discovered that he had metastasis of lung cancer. The cancer was winning and John was losing. Even in a wheelchair, with the large round surgical scar at the back of his head, he asked if we could take him to Mexico for one more warm winter holiday. Within a few days, our three children, spouses, teen grandson Marc, and my brother Ken were with him for a sunny vacation in Manzanillo, Mexico—one more time for him, as he wished!

He seemed so content to be there! One day, he surprised me by asking me to arrange a boat and a guide for a day to take the boys out fishing. They came back with a beautiful tuna and a dorado, which the chefs prepared and served at our dinner that night.

Another day, John asked me, "How come every time I open my eyes from a rest in our room, someone is always there, watching me?" I reminded him that earlier, when his care became palliative, he had said he never wanted to be alone, and with so much loving family, he never would be.

One of my tenderest memories is of my brother Ken sitting beside John in his wheelchair, facing the ocean, the two of them just sitting quietly, side by side, as the sun shone brightly on the little white boats in the calm blue waters of the bay and the happy noises of the resort surrounded them. John was enjoying one more special time, just as he wished ... being warm in winter.

My brother Ken beside John, enjoying John's last warm winter afternoon

Epilogue

Our family as we continued to live, love and laugh.

Charles, Karen, Kendra, with Marc and Hannah in front.

Laura and Allan.

Samantha, Sandy, Miranda, Keith.

Sandy and Keith, Laura and Al, me, Karen and Charles.

Grandpa built the dollhouse for the girls. Grandma made the nighties.

John lived two months more, being cared for at home, by the palliative care team and us. Keith and Sandy gave me a bunk bed so I could sleep beside John's hospital bed in our own room. All of our siblings came to visit with him. He continued to lose strength, but one late night, he reached for my neck and pulled me so close, so tight, it was like he was saying goodbye because the next morning on February 28, 2008, he took his last breath.

Printed in the USA
CPSIA information can be obtained
at www.ICGtesting.com
CBHW051455140624
10091CB00026B/386